VIRGINIA TEST PREP
Practice Test Book
SOL Reading
Grade 5

© 2018 by V. Hawas

All rights reserved. No part of this book may be reproduced or transmitted in any form or by any means, electronic, mechanical, photocopying, recording, or otherwise without prior written permission.

ISBN 978-1725652958

TEST MASTER PRESS

www.testmasterpress.com

CONTENTS

Introduction 4

Warm-Up Practice Tests 5

SOL Reading: Mini-Test 1   5
SOL Reading: Mini-Test 2   19
SOL Reading: Mini-Test 3   34

Complete Practice Tests 51

SOL Reading: Practice Test 1   51
SOL Reading: Practice Test 2   70
SOL Reading: Practice Test 3   88

Answer Key 108

SOL Reading: Mini-Test 1   109
SOL Reading: Mini-Test 2   111
SOL Reading: Mini-Test 3   113
SOL Reading: Practice Test 1   115
SOL Reading: Practice Test 2   117
SOL Reading: Practice Test 3   119

INTRODUCTION
For Parents, Teachers, and Tutors

About the SOL Reading Assessments

Students will be assessed each year by taking the SOL Reading assessments. This practice test book will prepare students for the assessments. It contains three warm-up tests that will introduce students to the types of tasks they will need to complete. This is followed by three full-length practice tests similar to the real SOL Reading tests.

About the Standards of Learning

In 2017, the state of Virginia adopted new *Standards of Learning*. The *Standards of Learning* describe what students are expected to know. All the exercises and questions in this book cover the *Standards of Learning* introduced in 2017.

Types of Tasks on the SOL Reading Assessments

The SOL Reading tests are taken online as computer adaptive tests. These tests contain several question types, including technology-enhanced items. The questions types are described below.

- Multiple-choice – students select the one correct answer from four possible options.
- Hot spot – students select one or more elements. An element could be a word, a phrase, a sentence, or an object.
- Hot text – students select text items from the passage. This may involve selecting phrases, sentences, or subtitles.
- Drag and drop – students drag one or more draggers to drop zones. Draggers could be words, phrases, sentences, or objects. These questions could involve completing a web or diagram, completing a table, or placing sentences in order.

This practice test book contains multiple-choice questions and questions with similar formats to the technology-enhanced items. To ensure that students develop strong reading comprehension skills, this book also contains written answer questions. These questions will give students the opportunity to analyze texts closely, explain their thinking, and use textual evidence to support conclusions and predictions.

Taking the Tests

The first three practice sets introduce students to the assessments with 25 questions that cover all the skills assessed and all the common question types. These short tests will allow students to become familiar with assessment questions before moving on to longer tests. These shorter tests may also be used as guided instruction before allowing students to complete the assessments on their own.

The remaining practice sets are complete full-length tests. Each practice test has 33 questions, which is the same as the actual SOL Reading test. By completing the practice tests, students will have ongoing practice with assessment items, develop the reading skills they need, gain experience with all types of test questions, and become fully prepared for the SOL Reading assessments.

SOL Reading

Mini-Test 1

Instructions

Read each passage and answer the questions that follow it.

For each multiple-choice question, fill in the circle for the correct answer. For other types of questions, follow the instructions given. Some of the questions require a written answer. Write your answer on the lines provided.

Tara's Fear

Tara was scared of flying. She always had been ever since she was a little girl. It hadn't been a problem for her as a child though, as her parents never took a vacation overseas. Despite this, Tara's fear grew steadily the older she got. She hated the idea of being up in the air and in flight.

One year her family announced that they would take their vacation abroad. They were going to New Zealand. Her father had planned an adventure trip that included white water rafting, fly fishing, and trekking up an old volcano. Tara had just turned 13 years old. Everything her father described sounded like the kind of great adventure she had only read about in books. She was excited by the thought of it all, but she couldn't stop thinking about the long flight there. She longed to go, but she didn't know if she could cope with the flight there. She was so distraught that she finally claimed that she simply could not go. As she lay crying on her bed at the thought, her father walked into her room.

"I can't do it, Dad," she said sobbing. "I won't be able to fly."

Her father placed his hand gently on her shoulder.

"I know honey," he whispered. "It's really difficult for you. I know exactly how you feel."

Tara looked up at her father. "Do you really?" she asked.

"When I was your age, I had a phobia too," he replied. "I never thought I'd ever get over it."

Tara sat upright on the bed. She would never have guessed that her father could be scared of anything.

"What were you scared of Dad?" she asked.

Her father looked at her before replying.

"It seems silly now, but I used to be scared of spiders. Whenever I saw one I would scream and run in the other direction. When I was young, I didn't even like playing outside because of spiders and small insects. One year my mother told me that we were going camping. I immediately refused to go. The idea of sleeping under the stars with all of those bugs scared the life out of me!"

"What happened then, Dad?" asked Tara.

"Well my mother talked to me," he replied. "She explained that she understood why I was scared, but that it was something that she could help me to overcome. Then she told me that once I did get over my fear, I would be able to enjoy being outdoors much more. She made me realize that I couldn't let a spider stop me from ever enjoying being outdoors. I had to focus on all the fun I would be having, not on the one thing that scared me."

A small smile crept across Tara's face.

"So did you go in the end then, Dad?" she asked.

"You bet I did," he replied without hesitation. "It was a challenge, but I kept thinking about my mother's words. They inspired me to face my fears. I went camping with my family and had the time of my life. You'll have the time of your life on our trip. You can't let your fear of the plane stop you from having all those good times. You just close your eyes and imagine yourself in New Zealand and don't let your fear take the good times away from you."

Tara suddenly felt determined. She was going to stand up to her fear and not let it steal her trip from her.

"Thanks Dad," said Tara. "You'd better make sure you book me a seat on the plane because I'm coming whether my fear likes it or not."

1 What does the word distraught mean in the sentence below?

She was so distraught that she finally claimed that she simply could not go.

- Ⓐ Disbelieving
- Ⓑ Distressed
- Ⓒ Uncertain
- Ⓓ Determined

2 In the sentence below, which word means about the same as steadily?

Despite this, Tara's fear grew steadily the older she got.

- Ⓐ Swiftly
- Ⓑ Weirdly
- Ⓒ Suddenly
- Ⓓ Gradually

3 How does Tara feel when her father first says that he had a phobia?

- Ⓐ Alarmed
- Ⓑ Surprised
- Ⓒ Excited
- Ⓓ Relieved

4 Based on the information in paragraph 2, explain why Tara has mixed feelings about the trip to New Zealand. Use details from the passage to explain your answer.

_____

_____

_____

_____

_____

_____

5 Read this sentence spoken by the father.

> **The idea of sleeping under the stars with all of those bugs scared the life out of me!**

Which literary device does the father use to emphasize how fearful he felt?

- Ⓐ Imagery, using details to create an image or picture
- Ⓑ Hyperbole, using exaggeration to make a point
- Ⓒ Simile, comparing two items using the words "like" or "as"
- Ⓓ Symbolism, using an object to stand for something else

6   Which statement best describes how you can tell that the passage is realistic fiction?

- Ⓐ   It has a theme that can be applied in real life.
- Ⓑ   It describes events that could really happen.
- Ⓒ   It has a modern setting.
- Ⓓ   It has a main problem.

7   How do the father's past experiences help him know how to help his daughter? Use details from the passage to support your answer.

_____

_____

_____

_____

_____

8   How are Tara and Tara's father similar?

- Ⓐ   They have the same fear of flying.
- Ⓑ   They have never flown before.
- Ⓒ   They receive help to overcome a fear from a parent.
- Ⓓ   They are thoughtful and understanding.

9 The main theme of the passage is about –

   Ⓐ admitting your fears

   Ⓑ letting other people help you

   Ⓒ not letting your fears hold you back

   Ⓓ making the most of every opportunity

10 Complete the cause and effect diagram below to show how Tara and Tara's father are affected by their fears.

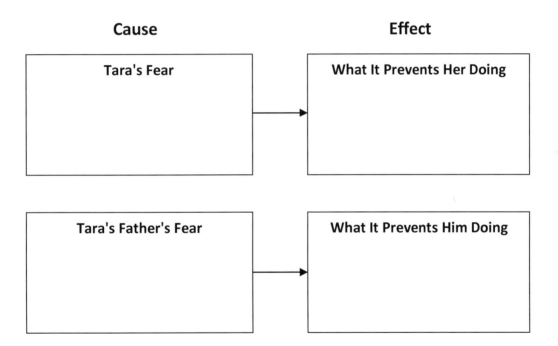

11 At the end of the passage, Tara says that she is going on the plane whether her fear likes it or not. Explain what Tara means by this.

_____

_____

_____

_____

_____

_____

12 In the passage, Tara wants to do the things her father has planned for them in New Zealand. Explain how this helps her be braver.

_____

_____

_____

_____

_____

_____

To My Teacher

June 15, 2017

Dear Miss Hooper,

I am writing to thank you for the help you have given me this year. We have covered many subjects in class and you have helped me with every single one. You explain things so clearly, and are also amazingly patient. I really believe you have a great skill for teaching others. Without your assistance, I would of struggled to do as well as I have. You should be very proud of the way that you help children to learn. It is because of you that I am thinking about becoming a teacher when I am older.

There were so many highlights this year. Whatever the subject, you made it fun and interesting to everyone. All of your students found learning new things so easy because of you. You never once made me feel silly for asking a question. You were always willing to explain something again and again until I understood.

I have mixed feelings about school next year. Firstly, I guess I am sad that you will no longer be my teacher. However, I am pleased that other children will get to share your knowledge. It would be selfish for me to keep you to myself all through school! I hope that they thank you for the good work that you do. You deserve it and it is the least we can do.

I did not enjoy school much before this year. I was new to the school this year. At my old school, I found learning difficult and quite a challenge. It made me so nervous about starting a new school, but the change turned out to be a huge blessing. The last nine months have changed everything. I am now very confident and looking forward to the next school year.

Thank you once again. You have truly been a great teacher and helped me greatly. I hope that we may even share the same classroom again one day.

Yours sincerely,

Jacob Maclean

13 Read this sentence from the letter.

> **There were so many highlights this year.**

What does the word <u>highlights</u> refer to?

- Ⓐ The best parts
- Ⓑ Challenges
- Ⓒ Breakthroughs
- Ⓓ Main ideas

14 Circle the **two** words from the passage that have about the same meaning.

help	pleased	interesting	selfish
fun	difficult	assistance	proud

15 Which sentence from the passage is a fact?

- Ⓐ *Whatever the subject, you made it fun and interesting to everyone.*
- Ⓑ *I really believe you have a great skill for teaching others.*
- Ⓒ *You should be very proud of the way that you help children to learn.*
- Ⓓ *I was new to the school this year.*

16 What is the main reason Jacob wrote the letter?

- Ⓐ To tell how he wants to become a teacher
- Ⓑ To explain that he is leaving the teacher's class
- Ⓒ To express his thanks to his teacher
- Ⓓ To encourage his teacher to keep working hard

17 Which sentence best summarizes the main idea of the letter?

- Ⓐ *It is because of you that I am thinking about becoming a teacher when I am older.*
- Ⓑ *I have mixed feelings about school next year.*
- Ⓒ *I did not enjoy school much before this year.*
- Ⓓ *You have truly been a great teacher and helped me greatly.*

18 Jacob describes Miss Hooper as "amazingly patient." Describe **two** details given in the passage that show her patience.

1: _____

_____

2: _____

_____

19 How does Jacob feel about not having Miss Hooper as his teacher next year?

- Ⓐ Upset and angry
- Ⓑ Pleased and excited
- Ⓒ Sad, but understanding
- Ⓓ Confused, but unconcerned

20 Based on your answer to Question 19, explain how you can tell that Jacob feels this way.

_____

_____

_____

_____

_____

_____

21 Which detail best explains why Jacob appreciates Miss Hooper so much?

- Ⓐ After this year, Jacob will not be taught by Miss Hooper.
- Ⓑ Before Miss Hooper, Jacob always found learning difficult.
- Ⓒ During the year, Jacob struggled more than all the other students.
- Ⓓ At his last school, Jacob was bored and made little effort.

22 Select **all** the statements that are effects Miss Hooper had on Jacob.

☐ Making him look forward to school next year

☐ Making him want to become a teacher

☐ Making him want to join more school clubs

☐ Helping him learn more

☐ Helping him make new friends

☐ Helping him become more confident

23 Jacob states that starting a new school "turned out to be a huge blessing." Explain why Jacob feels this way.

_____

_____

_____

_____

_____

24 Look at the chart below.

Why Jacob Thinks Miss Hooper is a Good Teacher

1) She is patient.
2)
3)

Complete the chart by writing **two** of the sentences in the empty spaces.

She is funny.   She is well-trained.   She explains things clearly.
She is proud.   She makes class fun.   She gives challenging work.

25 Read this paragraph from the passage.

> **Thank you once again. You have truly been a great teacher and helped me greatly. I hope that we may even share the same classroom again one day.**

How does this paragraph relate to the ideas of the rest of the passage?

- Ⓐ It introduces new ideas.
- Ⓑ It presents evidence against the main ideas.
- Ⓒ It restates the main ideas.
- Ⓓ It gives details to support the main ideas.

END OF PRACTICE TEST

SOL Reading

Mini-Test 2

Instructions

Read each passage and answer the questions that follow it.

For each multiple-choice question, fill in the circle for the correct answer. For other types of questions, follow the instructions given. Some of the questions require a written answer. Write your answer on the lines provided.

Playing a Musical Instrument

Playing a musical instrument is a popular pastime for all age ranges. Young or old, it is lots of fun to play a musical instrument. There are many different types to choose from including guitar, flute, piano, trumpet, and saxophone.

Making a Choice

First, you need to choose a musical instrument that you would like to learn how to play. Here are some things you should think about:

- the cost of the instrument
- how easy or difficult the instrument is to learn
- whether there is a teacher available to help you learn it
- what opportunities there will be to play it

You might also think about the kind of music you'd like to play. This will probably be the kind of music that you also enjoy listening to.

Another thing to consider is whether you'd like to play music alone or as part of a group. If you want to play alone, you might like to play the piano. This would not be a great choice if you'd like to play in a marching band! A trumpet or a trombone would be a better choice for that. If you'd like to play in a small group, you might choose the violin or the cello. String instruments like these are often played together in groups of two to four musicians. If you're imagining playing in a rock band, the guitar or the drums are popular choices. If you imagine yourself playing in a huge orchestra, you have lots of choices. You could play anything from the flute, to the saxophone, to the piano or the drums.

One other thing to consider is whether you would also like to sing as well. Some instruments are great for this, while others are not so good. It would be nearly impossible to sing while playing the trumpet! If you want to sing as well, consider learning the piano or the guitar. Just remember that you will have to work hard on your singing skills as well as your playing skills.

Getting Your Gear

Now you have chosen your instrument, you need to buy it. If it is expensive, you might like to borrow it instead. You might know a friend or relative who plays an instrument. You can ask to borrow an instrument for a little while to try it out. That way, you can make sure it is the right choice before spending lots of money. Some schools or libraries will lend students instruments. Or you can look in your local paper or online for a secondhand instrument.

Getting Ready to Learn

After you have your instrument, you should then create a learning plan. This might involve private lessons with a music teacher or going to music classes. Some people choose to learn on their own. You can use books, movies, web sites, or you can even watch videos online.

To learn quickly, your plan may include a variety of learning methods. Make sure that you attend every lesson or study your books regularly. Also, be sure to practice what you have learned as this is the best way to develop your new skill.

Making Music

Once you have learned enough to play a song, you should start playing for people. Many people get nervous when they first start performing. You might find that you make more mistakes than usual. Don't let this get you down. Remember that you will learn to calm and control your nerves the more you practice. It is often a good idea to start with your family or friends. Or you might play for your music class. Once you become confident, you can then play for larger groups of people.

Keep Going

To become a good musician, you have to keep playing. Keep learning as much as you can and practice often. Challenge yourself to learn more difficult songs as well. As you learn more, you will become better and better. Some people even become good enough to play music as a career.

1 Read this sentence from the passage.

> **Playing a musical instrument is a popular pastime for all age ranges.**

What does the word <u>pastime</u> mean?

Ⓐ   Choice

Ⓑ   Career

Ⓒ   Sport

Ⓓ   Hobby

2 According to the passage, what should you do first?

Ⓐ   Check to see if your school will lend you an instrument

Ⓑ   Decide what instrument you would like to play

Ⓒ   Create a plan for learning to play an instrument

Ⓓ   Look in your local newspaper for an instrument

3 Under which heading is information provided about deciding what type of instrument to learn to play? Circle the correct answer.

Making a Choice   Getting Your Gear

Getting Ready to Learn   Making Music   Keep Going

4   Read this sentence from the passage.

   Keep learning as much as you can and practice often.

   Which word means the opposite of <u>often</u>?
   - Ⓐ   Never
   - Ⓑ   Rarely
   - Ⓒ   More
   - Ⓓ   Regularly

5   The author provides the most information in the section "Making a Choice." Explain why you think this is such an important step. Give at least **two** reasons in your answer.

   _____

   _____

   _____

   _____

   _____

6   The web below lists ways that people can learn to play a musical instrument on their own.

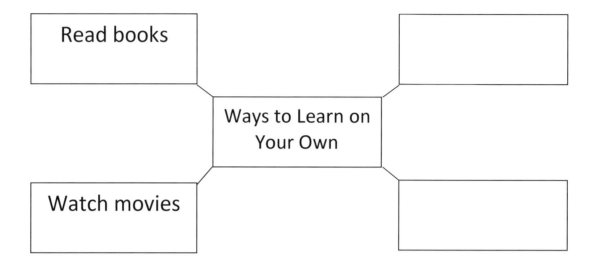

Which of these best complete the web? Write your answers in the web.

| Watch videos online | Find a tutor |
| Attend a class | Visit web sites |

7   What is the main purpose of the passage?

Ⓐ   To give readers guidance and advice

Ⓑ   To entertain readers with a story

Ⓒ   To teach people how to play a musical instrument

Ⓓ   To compare different musical instruments

8 Read this sentence from the section "Making Music."

It is a good idea to start with your family or friends.

Why does the author most likely suggest starting with your family or friends?

- Ⓐ So your friends will want to learn to play as well
- Ⓑ So your family will see that you are trying hard
- Ⓒ So you feel more comfortable playing
- Ⓓ So you can have people join in

9 Which sentence from "Making Music" best supports your answer to Question 8?

- Ⓐ *Many people get nervous when they first start performing.*
- Ⓑ *You might find that you make more mistakes than usual.*
- Ⓒ *Remember that you will learn to calm and control your nerves the more you practice.*
- Ⓓ *Or you might play for your music class.*

10 Why does the author use bullet points in the passage?

- Ⓐ To highlight the main points
- Ⓑ To list a set of ideas
- Ⓒ To show steps to follow in order
- Ⓓ To describe items that are needed

11 Complete the web below by listing **three** ways you could save money when getting a musical instrument.

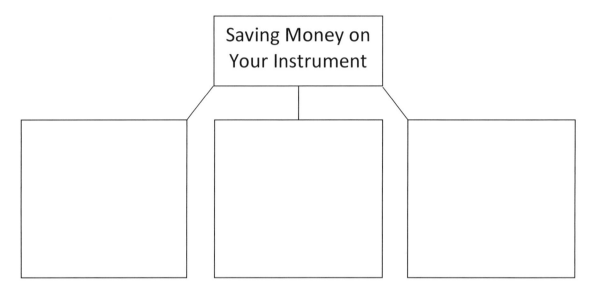

12 The photograph of the girl at the end of the passage is probably included to suggest which of the following?

- Ⓐ How much time and effort it takes to become good at playing
- Ⓑ How it is best to choose an instrument you can play on your own
- Ⓒ How enjoyable and rewarding playing an instrument is
- Ⓓ How it can be difficult to play for an audience at first

13   Complete the graphic organizer below by listing **two** instruments that would be suitable for each purpose.

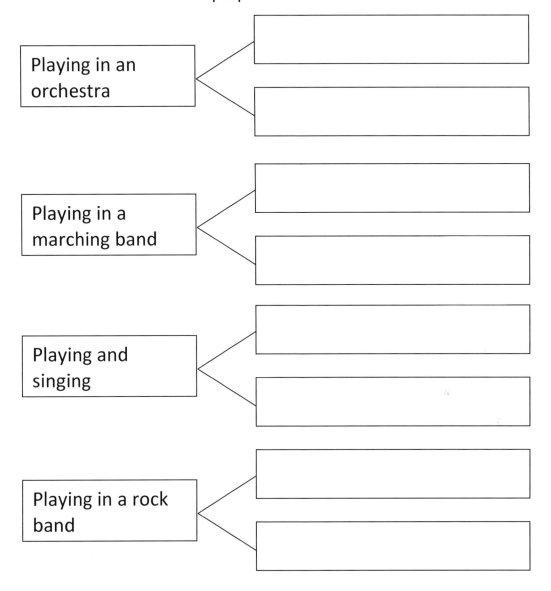

The Bees, the Wasps, and the Hornet

A store of honey had been found in a hollow tree. The wasps stated that it belonged to them. The bees were just as sure that the treasure was theirs. The argument grew very heated. It looked as if the affair could not be settled. But at last, with much good sense, they agreed to let a judge decide the matter. They brought the case before Judge Hornet.

When Judge Hornet called the case, witnesses stated that they had seen certain winged creatures in the neighborhood of the hollow tree. The creatures had hummed loudly, had striped bodies, and were yellow and black.

The wasps stated that this described them. The bees stated that this described them.

This did not help Judge Hornet make a decision. He said he wanted to take a few days to think about the case. When the case came up again, both sides had a large number of witnesses.

Judge Hornet sighed. He knew it was going to be a long day. Then the eldest bee asked if he could address the court.

"I'll allow it," Judge Hornet said.

"Your honor," the eldest bee said, "the case has now been going on for a week. If it is not decided soon, the honey will not be fit for anything. I move that the bees and the wasps be both instructed to make some honey. Then we shall soon see to whom the honey really belongs."

The wasps began to panic. They jumped up and down and complained loudly. Wise Judge Hornet quickly understood why they did so.

"It is clear," said Judge Hornet, "who made the honey and who could not have made it. The honey belongs to the bees."

14 Read this sentence from the passage.

The argument grew very heated.

The word <u>heated</u> suggests that the bees and wasps became –

- Ⓐ confused
- Ⓑ angry
- Ⓒ warm
- Ⓓ tired

15 In the sentence below, why does the author use the word <u>treasure</u>?

The bees were just as sure that the treasure was theirs.

- Ⓐ To suggest that the honey was gold
- Ⓑ To show that the honey was hidden
- Ⓒ To show that the honey had been there a long time
- Ⓓ To suggest that the honey was precious

16 What is the main purpose of the first paragraph?

- Ⓐ To describe the main problem
- Ⓑ To compare the bees and the wasps
- Ⓒ To introduce the setting
- Ⓓ To describe how to solve an argument

17 The main lesson the wasps learn is about being –

- Ⓐ hardworking
- Ⓑ honest
- Ⓒ prepared
- Ⓓ skilled

18 Based on your answer to Question 17, explain how the outcome for the wasps shows the main lesson.

_____

_____

_____

_____

_____

19 How is the passage mainly organized?

- Ⓐ Two events are compared and contrasted.
- Ⓑ Events are described in the order they occur.
- Ⓒ Facts are given to support an argument.
- Ⓓ A question is asked and then answered.

20 Why do the wasps most likely panic when the elder bee suggests that the judge should instruct the bees and wasps to make honey?

- Ⓐ The wasps know they cannot make honey.
- Ⓑ The wasps are too tired to make honey.
- Ⓒ The wasps think the bees' honey will taste better.
- Ⓓ The wasps think it will take too long.

21 Explain what the judge decides when he sees the wasps panicking. Explain how the wasps' actions cause the judge to reach his decision.

_____

_____

_____

_____

_____

_____

22 Based on his suggestion, the eldest bee is best described as –

- Ⓐ impatient
- Ⓑ polite
- Ⓒ wise
- Ⓓ cranky

23   The passage states that "when the case came up again, both sides had a large number of witnesses." How does this influence the events?

   Ⓐ   It makes the wasps sorry for their actions because they realize how much the bees care about the honey.

   Ⓑ   It makes the wasps upset and nervous because they fear being embarrassed in front of so many people.

   Ⓒ   It makes the judge want to be sure to make the right decision because he knows how important it must be to both sides.

   Ⓓ   It makes the judge open to listening to the ideas of the eldest bee because the judge wants to find a faster solution.

24   Complete the table below by describing **one** way the bees and the wasps are similar and **one** way the bees and the wasps are different. In the second column, describe how the similarity or difference affects the events of the passage.

Similarity	Effect on the Events
Difference	Effect on the Events

25 What is the main problem in the passage? How is the main problem solved? Use details from the passage to support your answer.

_____

_____

_____

_____

_____

END OF PRACTICE TEST

SOL Reading

Mini-Test 3

Instructions

Read each passage and answer the questions that follow it.

For each multiple-choice question, fill in the circle for the correct answer. For other types of questions, follow the instructions given. Some of the questions require a written answer. Write your answer on the lines provided.

The Lighthouse

Simon was fascinated with the lighthouse to the south of the island. It was just two miles from his front door. The lighthouse stood proudly above the sea and cast its light for miles. It had stood in that spot for over two hundred years. Wind and rain had battered it, but the lighthouse stood strong and sturdy. During the day, you could see the aging of the old stone bricks.

Simon often stared at the lighthouse and wondered about its history. He had even heard rumors that it was haunted by a stonemason that had helped build it. He had been told the stonemason's initials were carved into some of the stones. Simon had never been close enough to see it for himself. At night it was an eerie presence. The white stones shone in the moonlight like a ghost hovering over the sea. Simon knew the lighthouse was meant to protect sailors. But sometimes he felt like it was watching him. Simon and his friends were scared to even go near it.

One night, Rick was staying at Simon's house. Just like Simon, he couldn't help stare at the lighthouse.

"I think we should head over there," said Rick, who was Simon's best friend. He was always more adventurous than his sensible friend.

Simon thought carefully before responding.

"But aren't you scared?" he asked.

"Not at all. Are you?" Rick replied.

Simon did not want to look scared in front of his best friend.

"No," he replied nervously.

"That is settled then," said Rick. "We will head out this evening."

After dinner, they gathered some food and supplies and packed them into Rick's backpack. Then they headed out toward the lighthouse. Both boys were very quiet as they walked through the fields on the island.

"You're not saying much," said Simon. "Are you okay?"

"I'm fine," said Rick. "I was just thinking."

When they reached the shore, the sun was starting to set above the sea. The boys slowly climbed the small rock face as the sun went down. They both stopped as they stood in front of the lighthouse door.

"In you go then Simon," said Rick, gesturing toward the wooden door.

"You go first," said Simon. "It was your idea."

Rick paused and didn't say a single word. Then Rick edged toward the door. He stopped and looked back at Simon, who gave a small nod of encouragement. He arrived at the step and reached out for the door handle. Simon had stayed back in the shadows. As Rick twisted the handle, he suddenly heard a loud growling from inside.

"Run!" shouted Rick at the top of his voice.

He raced away, with Simon following close behind him. They ran back to the main road and headed back toward Simon's house. Rick looked very sheepish as they made their way home.

"Didn't you want to see inside?" asked Simon.

Rick shrugged and looked down at the ground.

"I guess it was scarier than I thought," he whispered.

"Oh, I don't know," said Simon. "It wasn't that bad."

1   Read this sentence from the passage.

    At night it was an eerie presence.

    Circle **all** the words that have about the same meaning as <u>eerie</u>.

    creepy   amusing   ghostly   useful

    gigantic   scary   calming   welcoming

2   Select the **three** details given about the lighthouse that best explain why Simon finds it eerie. Tick **three** boxes to show your choices.

    ☐   Simon is fascinated by it.

    ☐   It is two miles from Simon's house.

    ☐   It stands proudly above the sea.

    ☐   It casts its light for miles.

    ☐   It is two hundred years old.

    ☐   It is made of white stones that seem to shine at night.

    ☐   There are rumors that it is haunted.

    ☐   Simon has never been near it.

    ☐   Its job is to protect sailors.

    ☐   Simon feels like it is watching him.

3   Read this sentence from the passage.

    Then Rick edged toward the door.

    The word <u>edged</u> shows that Rick moved –
    - Ⓐ swiftly
    - Ⓑ slowly
    - Ⓒ suddenly
    - Ⓓ smoothly

4   Based on your answer to Question 3, what does the way Rick moves show about how he feels? Use details from the passage in your answer.

    _____

    _____

    _____

    _____

    _____

5   Which statement is most likely true about Rick?

- Ⓐ   He is not scared of anything.
- Ⓑ   He is not as fearless as he says he is.
- Ⓒ   He enjoys seeing how scared Simon is.
- Ⓓ   He only pretends to be frightened.

6   Which word in the sentence below shows that the author is using personification?

> **The lighthouse stood proudly above the sea and cast its light for miles.**

- Ⓐ   *proudly*
- Ⓑ   *above*
- Ⓒ   *light*
- Ⓓ   *miles*

7   Why does Rick tell Simon to run?

- Ⓐ   He sees a creature inside the lighthouse.
- Ⓑ   He hears a noise from inside the lighthouse.
- Ⓒ   He thinks they are going to get in trouble for being inside the lighthouse.
- Ⓓ   He realizes that the owner of the lighthouse is home.

8 At the start of the passage, Rick says that he is not scared of going to the lighthouse. Describe **two** details that suggest that Rick is more scared than he admits.

1: _____

_____

2: _____

_____

9 What is the point of view in the passage?

Ⓐ First person

Ⓑ Second person

Ⓒ Third person limited

Ⓓ Third person omniscient

10 According to the passage, how is Simon different from Rick?

Ⓐ He is more sensible.

Ⓑ He is more adventurous.

Ⓒ He is more intelligent.

Ⓓ He is more determined.

11 Read this sentence from the passage.

Rick shrugged and looked down at the ground.

The author uses this description to suggest that Rick feels –

Ⓐ angry

Ⓑ embarrassed

Ⓒ amused

Ⓓ terrified

12 Circle the word below that you think best describes Simon. Explain why you made that choice.

brave   cowardly

_____

_____

_____

_____

_____

13 In the first two paragraphs below, the author gives details about the lighthouse. Complete the table by listing **three** examples of factual details and **three** examples of Simon's personal opinions or feelings.

Simon was fascinated with the lighthouse to the south of the island. It was just two miles from his front door. The lighthouse stood proudly above the sea and cast its light for miles. It had stood in that spot for over two hundred years. Wind and rain had battered it, but the lighthouse stood strong and sturdy. During the day, you could see the aging of the old stone bricks.

Simon often stared at the lighthouse and wondered about its history. He had even heard rumors that it was haunted by a stonemason that had helped build it. He had been told the stonemason's initials were carved into some of the stones. Simon had never been close enough to see it for himself. At night it was an eerie presence. The white stones shone in the moonlight like a ghost hovering over the sea. Simon knew the lighthouse was meant to protect sailors. But sometimes he felt like it was watching him. Simon and his friends were scared to even go near it.

Factual Details	Simon's Opinions or Feelings

Manchester United Soccer Club

About Soccer

1. Soccer is a ball sport that was invented in England in the 1800s. It is an outdoor sport. An individual match sees two teams of 11 players compete against each other. The object of the game is to work the ball into one of the two goals positioned at each end of the field.

2. It is a sport that is played all over the world. It is most popular in South America and Europe. The most successful international team is Brazil. They have won five World Cups since 1930, which is a competition that is held every 4 years. Italy has won four World Cups. Germany is not far behind, with three wins.

3. Soccer is not as popular as sports like baseball and football in the United States. The 2013 championship match of Major League Soccer in America had a crowd of 21,650. This is much less than for the Super Bowl, which had 71,000 people. However, soccer is a very entertaining sport to watch. Soccer may become a favorite sport in the United States one day.

4. As with popular American sports, major teams enjoy the massive support of their fans. Manchester United Soccer Club is based in the United Kingdom and is one of the most-loved teams. The love that fans have of the team is based on their long history, their success, and the talented and popular players that have been part of the team.

A Famous Soccer Club

5. Manchester United is a famous soccer team. They are based in the United Kingdom. They play in the English Premier League and the European Champions League. They are known as one of the most successful soccer clubs in the world.

6. They were first formed in 1888. At this time, they were named the Newton Heath Football Club. In 1901, they were sold and were given the new name of Manchester United.

7. They are the most successful club in the English League. They have won the English Premier League nineteen times. This is one more than their nearest rivals, Liverpool.

8. Since 1958, Manchester United have also won the European Champions League three times. This competition features teams from across Europe. It is this success that has helped them become such a well-known team.

9. David Beckham is one of the club's most famous players. He played for Manchester United from 1993 until 2003. In this time, he scored 62 goals for the club and helped his team win eight championships. He scored some amazing goals, including one from the halfway line that floated above the goalkeeper's head and curved into the net. The goal became so famous that it was voted by the British public as number 18 on a list of 100 greatest sporting moments. Beckham was known for being able to curve or bend the ball. It allowed him to score some amazing goals. These thrilled fans and helped draw huge crowds to games.

©Wikimedia Commons

10. In 2007, Beckham made an unexpected move. He joined America's Major League Soccer, and began playing for Los Angeles Galaxy. He was paid around $6.5 million per year. One of the most interesting things about the deal was that Beckham was not just paid by the Los Angeles Galaxy team. He was also paid by all the teams in America's Major League Soccer. The teams agreed to this because they hoped that having such a major star in their league would attract more people to the sport.

Manchester United's English Premier League Grand Final Wins

Year	Team Defeated
1908	Aston Villa
1911	Aston Villa
1952	Tottenham
1956	Blackpool
1957	Tottenham
1965	Leeds United
1967	Nottingham Forest
1993	Aston Villa
1994	Blackburn Rovers
1996	Newcastle United
1997	Newcastle United
1999	Arsenal
2000	Arsenal
2001	Arsenal
2003	Arsenal
2007	Chelsea
2008	Chelsea
2009	Chelsea
2011	Chelsea

14 Which meaning of the word <u>object</u> is used in the sentence below?

The object of the game is to work the ball into one of the two goals positioned at each end of the field.

- Ⓐ A goal or aim
- Ⓑ A type of item
- Ⓒ To argue against
- Ⓓ To refuse to do something

15 Which detail from the passage is an opinion?

- Ⓐ Soccer was invented in the 1800s.
- Ⓑ Soccer is an outdoor sport.
- Ⓒ Soccer teams have 11 players each.
- Ⓓ Soccer is entertaining to watch.

16 Complete the table by adding information about the **three** most successful international teams. Order the teams from most to least successful.

Most Successful International Teams	Number of World Cup Wins Since 1930
1.	
2.	
3.	

17 Where was the game of soccer invented?

   Ⓐ England

   Ⓑ Brazil

   Ⓒ Italy

   Ⓓ Germany

18 Draw lines to match each sentence in paragraph 3 with the best description of the sentence. The first sentence has been matched for you.

Sentence	Description
Soccer is not as popular as sports like baseball and football in the United States.	a prediction
The 2013 championship match of Major League Soccer in America had a crowd of 21,650.	the main claim
This is much less than for the Super Bowl, which had 71,000 people.	an opinion
However, soccer is a very entertaining sport to watch.	a comparison
Soccer may become a favorite sport in the United States one day.	a fact given to support a claim

(The first sentence is matched to "the main claim".)

19 Circle the **two** words from the passage that have about the same meaning.

formed   rivals   success   competition

famous   teams   named   well-known

20 Which sentence is best supported by the information in the table at the end of the passage?

Ⓐ *They have won the English Premier League nineteen times.*

Ⓑ *This is one more than their nearest rivals, Liverpool.*

Ⓒ *Since 1958, Manchester United have also won the European Champions League three times.*

Ⓓ *This competition features teams from across Europe.*

21 Write F next to the sentences that are facts. Write O next to the sentences that are opinions.

___ They are based in the United Kingdom.

___ In 1901, they were sold and were given the new name of Manchester United.

___ Since 1958, Manchester United have also won the European Champions League three times.

___ It is this success that has helped them become such a well-known team.

22 List **two** facts the author includes to show that Manchester United have been a successful team.

1: _____

_____

2: _____

_____

23 Paragraph 10 describes how David Beckham was paid by all the teams in America's Major League Soccer. Which idea from "About Soccer" does this detail best support?

- Ⓐ Soccer is played all over the world.
- Ⓑ Soccer is not as popular in America as other sports.
- Ⓒ Soccer teams in Europe enjoy massive support from their fans.
- Ⓓ Soccer is played by teams of 11 players.

24 What is the main purpose of the seventh and eighth paragraphs?

- Ⓐ To describe how the team formed
- Ⓑ To describe the team's achievements
- Ⓒ To explain why the team is successful
- Ⓓ To show that the team has improved over time

25. Read this dictionary entry for the word <u>deal</u>.

> **deal** *noun*
> 1. a business agreement 2. a bargain 3. the treatment given to somebody 4. the distribution of cards

Now read this sentence from the passage.

> **One of the most interesting things about the deal was that Beckham was not just paid by the Los Angeles Galaxy team.**

Which definition of the word <u>deal</u> is used in the sentence above?

Ⓐ Definition 1
Ⓑ Definition 2
Ⓒ Definition 3
Ⓓ Definition 4

END OF PRACTICE TEST

SOL Reading

Practice Test 1

Instructions

Read each passage and answer the questions that follow it.

For each multiple-choice question, fill in the circle for the correct answer. For other types of questions, follow the instructions given. Some of the questions require a written answer. Write your answer on the lines provided.

A New Arrival

Today was a very exciting day for me and my family. It was the day that my new baby brother came home from the hospital.

I remember when I first learned that I was going to have a new baby brother. "I have great news Emma," my mother said. "You are going to be a big sister." I just stared at my mother and I didn't even smile. I really wasn't sure what to think, but I had all these thoughts running through my head. I worried that he would drive me crazy by crying all the time. I worried that my parents might want him to have my room. I even worried that Mom would be too busy to come and watch me at my dance competitions.

All those things I worried about seem ridiculous now. I soon forgot about most of them anyway. By the time he was ready to arrive, I didn't have a single worry. I was far too excited about getting to meet him. I was looking forward to being his big sister and helping to look after him.

My baby brother was born yesterday morning at 9:51. My father came home in the afternoon and was overjoyed. He weighed 8 pounds and 1 ounce and my parents named him Bradley. My dad says that he is the most beautiful baby. I could barely sleep the night before. I was so excited about Bradley coming home. Eventually, I drifted off to sleep just as the morning sun began to rise.

I woke up as usual today at 9 o'clock. I went downstairs and enjoyed some toast for breakfast. I knew that my father was collecting my mother and Bradley at 11:30. I watched TV for a while before trying to read one of my favorite books. Whatever I tried to do, I just could not take my mind off my newborn brother. I couldn't help but try to imagine what he must look like. In my mind, he had bright blond hair and sparkling blue eyes. I wondered whether he would understand who I was when he first saw me. My daydreaming was interrupted by my dad's voice. "Let's go Emma," he called. It was finally time to leave.

I headed out to the car and we drove toward the hospital. I couldn't stop talking as we made our way through the winding roads. The short trip to the hospital seemed to take forever. We finally arrived at the hospital. We made our way through the reception and headed to the maternity ward. As we arrived at the doors, I could see my mother at the far end. She held a small bundle wrapped in a blue blanket in her arms.

Mom just smiled as I reached the end of her bed. She looked tired but extremely happy. I just stared for a few moments before Mom asked me if I wanted to meet my brother! I couldn't stop smiling and reached out in an instant. Mom held out her arms and passed Bradley to me.

I took him in my arms and cradled his tiny little baby body. As I looked down, he slowly opened his eyes and gazed up at me. They were the deepest blue that anyone could ever imagine. As I stroked his face he began to smile softly. Dad told me that he looks just like me when I was born. The thought that I was ever that beautiful made me smile. Then Bradley slowly closed his eyes and drifted off to sleep.

1   Which word best describes the tone of the sentence below?

    I took him in my arms and cradled his tiny little baby body.

    Ⓐ   Loving

    Ⓑ   Casual

    Ⓒ   Lively

    Ⓓ   Serious

2   Which word means about the same as <u>overjoyed</u>?

    My father came home in the afternoon and was overjoyed.

    Ⓐ   Tired

    Ⓑ   Delighted

    Ⓒ   Relaxed

    Ⓓ   Gloomy

3   Why does Emma most likely say that the trip to the hospital "seemed to take forever"?

    Ⓐ   Her father got lost on the way.

    Ⓑ   She was nervous about seeing her brother.

    Ⓒ   She was excited and impatient.

    Ⓓ   She lived far from the hospital.

4 Read this sentence from the passage.

They were the deepest blue that anyone could ever imagine.

Which literary device is used in the sentence?

- Ⓐ Alliteration, using words with the same consonant sounds
- Ⓑ Hyperbole, using exaggeration to make a point
- Ⓒ Simile, comparing two items using the words "like" or "as"
- Ⓓ Symbolism, using an object to stand for something else

5 Which of these would Emma probably most look forward to doing the next day?

- Ⓐ Reading her favorite book
- Ⓑ Chatting with her father
- Ⓒ Watching television
- Ⓓ Rocking her brother to sleep

6 Which **two** words would Emma most likely use to describe her day? Tick the boxes of the words you have chosen.

- ☐ eerie   ☐ surprising
- ☐ annoying   ☐ disappointing
- ☐ special   ☐ dull
- ☐ strange   ☐ unforgettable

7   Which paragraph contains a flashback to a past time? Circle your choice. Then explain the purpose of the flashback.

   Paragraph 1   Paragraph 2   Paragraph 3   Paragraph 4

   Paragraph 5   Paragraph 6   Paragraph 7   Paragraph 8

   _____

   _____

   _____

   _____

   _____

8   How can you tell that the author is excited about having a baby brother? Use at least **two** details from the passage in your answer.

   _____

   _____

   _____

   _____

   _____

9   Emma's first reaction to finding out she is going to have a brother can be described as selfish. List **two** details from the passage that show this.

1: _____

_____

2: _____

_____

10 Complete the web below by adding **three** more phrases from the paragraph below that create a sense of calm.

> **I took him in my arms and cradled his tiny little baby body. As I looked down, he slowly opened his eyes and gazed up at me. They were the deepest blue that anyone could ever imagine. As I stroked his face he began to smile softly. Dad told me that he looks just like me when I was born. The thought that I was ever that beautiful made me smile. Then Bradley slowly closed his eyes and drifted off to sleep.**

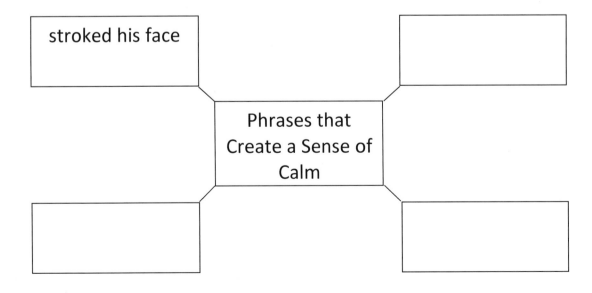

Writing a Short Story
By Kevin Baker

Writing a short story is a popular and satisfying hobby for a lot of people. It is also an excellent way to express creative thoughts. Writing a good story is not easy, but it is certainly worth the effort. Here are the steps to take to write a good story.

Step 1

Every story starts with an idea. Start by thinking about the things that you enjoy. These activities are excellent subjects to base your stories on. Other ideas can come from thinking about subjects that you'd like to know more about.

Step 2

Once you have an idea, you can then decide who your main characters are going to be. Consider having both a hero and a villain in your story. This will help to keep your readers interested. A hero is also known as a protagonist, while a villain is known as an antagonist. You'll also need to think of the best location for your story to take place.

Step 3

Before you start writing, you need to plan your story. Most writers plan their stories by creating an outline. An outline is like an overview of the story. It should describe the main events that occur. Your story should have a beginning, a middle, and an end. This will help anyone who reads the story to follow its events.

Step 4

Now that you have your outline, it is time to start writing. Follow your outline and write your story. At this point, your story does not have to be perfect. You will go back and improve it later.

Step 5

The story you have written is your first draft. The next step is to read through it and revise it. Here are some questions to help you decide what might need to be changed:

- Are the events that happen clear?
- Is the story interesting?
- Have I described the characters well?
- Can I use better descriptions to make it more exciting?
- Have I left out any important points?
- Is the start of the story good enough to get the reader interested?
- Would the ending leave the reader feeling satisfied?

Keep working on your story until it is the best you can make it.

Step 6

Once the story is complete, read it in full to ensure that it is well-written and easy to follow. Make sure that all your sentences flow well and are easy to understand. You should also check for any spelling or grammar mistakes.

Step 7

It is now time to get some feedback on your story. Have others read your story so that they can make suggestions for improvements. Think about the advice that people tell you. You do not have to take all the advice given, but you should think about it.

Step 8

Revise your story again based on the feedback you have been given. You should also read through it again to make sure all your sentences are written correctly and to ensure that there are no spelling or grammar errors.

You should now have a well-written, polished, and entertaining story.

11 Read this sentence from the passage.

   You should now have a well-written, polished, and entertaining story.

   What does the word <u>polished</u> show about the story?
   - Ⓐ It is enjoyable to read.
   - Ⓑ It is smooth and free from errors.
   - Ⓒ It has been well-planned.
   - Ⓓ It has a suitable ending.

12 Based on your answer to Question 11, choose the **two** steps that will most ensure that the story is polished. Circle the steps you have chosen. Then explain why you chose those steps.

   Step 1   Step 2   Step 3   Step 4

   Step 5   Step 6   Step 7   Step 8

   _____
   _____
   _____
   _____
   _____

13 Read this sentence from the passage.

> **It is also an excellent way to express creative thoughts.**

Which meaning of the word <u>express</u> is used in the sentence?

- Ⓐ To send something quickly
- Ⓑ To put into words
- Ⓒ Plain or clear
- Ⓓ Direct or fast

14 What does the transition phrase in the sentence below show about how the sentence is organized?

> **Before you start writing, you need to plan your story.**

- Ⓐ It gives a cause and its effect.
- Ⓑ It states a main idea and a supporting detail.
- Ⓒ It compares and contrast two ideas.
- Ⓓ It tells the sequence or order.

15 What is the main purpose of the passage?

- Ⓐ To teach readers how to do something
- Ⓑ To encourage people to read more
- Ⓒ To explain the purpose of writing
- Ⓓ To compare different types of hobbies

16 Why does the author use bullet points in the passage?

- Ⓐ To highlight the main points
- Ⓑ To list a set of ideas
- Ⓒ To show steps to follow in order
- Ⓓ To describe items that are needed

17 In which step is the first draft of the story written? Circle the correct step.

Step 1   Step 2   Step 3   Step 4

Step 5   Step 6   Step 7   Step 8

18 Explain what the terms <u>protagonist</u> and <u>antagonist</u> mean. Explain why you think having both in the story would help keep the reader interested.

_____

_____

_____

_____

_____

19   According to the passage, what should you do first when writing a story?

- Ⓐ   Decide who the main character is going to be
- Ⓑ   Write an outline of the story
- Ⓒ   Discuss your story idea with other people
- Ⓓ   Think of an idea for the story

20   The author states that "writing a good story is not easy." How does the information in the passage support this statement? Use details from the passage in your answer.

_____

_____

_____

_____

_____

_____

Little White Lily
By George Macdonald

1. Little White Lily
Sat by a stone,
Drooping and waiting
Till the sun shone.

2. Little White Lily
Sunshine has fed;
Little White Lily
Is lifting her head.

3. Little White Lily
Said: "It is good
Little White Lily's
Clothing and food."

4. Little White Lily
Dressed like a bride!
Shining with whiteness,
And crowned beside!

5. Little White Lily
Drooping with pain,
Waiting and waiting
For the wet rain.

6. Little White Lily
Holdeth her cup;
Rain is fast falling
And filling it up.

7. Little White Lily
Said: "Good again,
When I am thirsty
To have the nice rain.

8. Now I am stronger,
Now I am cool;
Heat cannot burn me,
My veins are so full."

9. Little White Lily
Smells very sweet;
On her head sunshine,
Rain at her feet.

10. Thanks to the sunshine,
Thanks to the rain,
Little White Lily
Is happy again.

21 Read these lines from the poem.

> **Little White Lily**
> **Is happy again.**

Which literary device does the poet use in these lines?

Ⓐ Simile

Ⓑ Metaphor

Ⓒ Personification

Ⓓ Hyperbole

22 Based on your answer to Question 21, explain how the literary device helps readers connect with the poem.

_____

_____

_____

_____

_____

23   Based on the poem, what is most important to the lily?

   Ⓐ   Having water

   Ⓑ   Smelling nice

   Ⓒ   Being appreciated

   Ⓓ   Getting shelter

24   What is the rhyme pattern of each stanza of the poem?

   Ⓐ   The second and fourth lines rhyme.

   Ⓑ   There are two pairs of rhyming lines.

   Ⓒ   The first and last lines rhyme.

   Ⓓ   None of the lines rhyme.

25   Select **all** the lines below that contain alliteration.

   ☐   *Sat by a stone,*

   ☐   *Drooping and waiting*

   ☐   *Sunshine has fed;*

   ☐   *Shining with whiteness,*

   ☐   *Rain is fast falling*

   ☐   *Heat cannot burn me,*

   ☐   *Thanks to the rain,*

26 Which of the following is used throughout the poem?

　Ⓐ　Symbolism, using an object to stand for something else

　Ⓑ　Hyperbole, using exaggeration to make a point

　Ⓒ　Repetition, repeating words, phrases, or lines

　Ⓓ　Flashback, referring back to an event in the past

27 Why does the poet compare the lily to a bride?

　Ⓐ　To show how special the lily feels

　Ⓑ　To emphasize how white the lily is

　Ⓒ　To explain that the lily is being used in a wedding

　Ⓓ　To suggest that the lily moves slowly

28 Read these lines from the poem.

　　Little White Lily
　　Drooping with pain,
　　Waiting and waiting
　　For the wet rain.

　These lines suggest that the lily feels –

　Ⓐ　confident

　Ⓑ　desperate

　Ⓒ　calm

　Ⓓ　angry

29 In which stanza does the lily feel about the same as in the first stanza? Circle the stanza you have chosen.

   Stanza 2   Stanza 3   Stanza 4   Stanza 5   Stanza 6

   Stanza 7   Stanza 8   Stanza 9   Stanza 10

30 Think about how the lily feels in the first stanza and the stanza you identified in Question 29. Compare and contrast why the lily feels that way in each stanza.

   _____
   _____
   _____
   _____
   _____
   _____
   _____

31 The poet probably uses the word <u>drooping</u> in the first paragraph to create a sense of –

   Ⓐ   determination
   Ⓑ   sadness
   Ⓒ   loneliness
   Ⓓ   relaxation

32   Read these lines from the poem.

> **Little White Lily**
> **Holdeth her cup;**
> **Rain is fast falling**
> **And filling it up.**

Explain what these lines are describing. Why can what is described not happen until the sun is shining?

_____

_____

_____

_____

33   Complete the table below by listing **two** stanzas that include dialogue. For each stanza, describe what the dialogue tells the reader.

Stanza	What the Dialogue Tells the Reader

END OF PRACTICE TEST

SOL Reading

Practice Test 2

Instructions

Read each passage and answer the questions that follow it.

For each multiple-choice question, fill in the circle for the correct answer. For other types of questions, follow the instructions given. Some of the questions require a written answer. Write your answer on the lines provided.

The River Bank Creative Writing Group

Creative writing is a great way of expressing yourself. The problem is that many people never try to write. Many people believe that they do not have the ability. At the River Bank Creative Writing Group, we aim to unleash your creativity.

We are based in Brooklyn, New York. We started our community organization in the fall of 2001. In the years since then, we have brought creative writing into the lives of many local residents. It does not matter whether you wish to write creatively as a hobby or as a way of making money. We have experienced and skilled staff to help you achieve success. We start by teaching the very basics of creative writing. Then we develop a program that is unique to your skills and goals. This can focus on writing short stories, poetry, plays, or anything else that interests you.

So what exactly do we offer? Well, our creative workshops are known for their quality. Our teachers include experienced professional writers and editors. They will guide you and help you get started. They will also offer feedback on your writing to help you improve. We also have guest speakers who attend once a week and share their own advice and experience. These are usually published authors who have achieved success in their fields. Our guest list is varied and includes successful poets, short story writers, and novelists. Their practical experience is the key to unlocking your creative talents.

We have achieved some great results at the River Bank Creative Writing Group. In 2005, one of our earliest students had her first novel published. She has since gone on to enjoy two further publications and is known worldwide. In 2009, another of our writers had his first poetry collection published. Thousands of our other writers have emerged from our classes as skilled creative writers.

Our classes can benefit you regardless of your goals. If you wish to unlock your creative skill for an exciting pastime, then we can help you. If you dream of being a published author, then we can help you make that happen. It has never been easier to unlock your creativity. If you have an interest in creative writing, then contact us today. We are waiting to hear from you and ready to help you on your journey!

1   In the sentence below, what does the word <u>unleash</u> mean?

At the River Bank Creative Writing Group, we aim to unleash your creativity.

- Ⓐ   Take control of
- Ⓑ   Train and shape
- Ⓒ   Set free
- Ⓓ   Benefit from

2   What is the main purpose of the fourth paragraph?

- Ⓐ   To encourage people to take writing seriously
- Ⓑ   To show the success of the writing group
- Ⓒ   To describe different types of writing styles
- Ⓓ   To suggest that getting published is easy

3   Describe **two** details given in the fourth paragraph that support your answer to Question 2.

1: _____

_____

2: _____

_____

4   What does the picture at the end of the passage most likely symbolize?

   Ⓐ   How long the writing group has existed for

   Ⓑ   How much of an achievement writing a book could be

   Ⓒ   How the teachers at the group are very experienced

   Ⓓ   How the writing group offers a range of services

5   From the information in the passage, the reader can conclude that the writing group –

   Ⓐ   is mainly for young writers

   Ⓑ   offers the services for free

   Ⓒ   is suited to all types of writers

   Ⓓ   considers publishing writers' works

6   The passage was probably written mainly to –

   Ⓐ   encourage people to attend the writing group's classes

   Ⓑ   highlight the benefits of creative writing

   Ⓒ   describe the history of the creative writing group

   Ⓓ   convince successful writers to be guest speakers

7   Complete the chart below by listing **three** ways the River Bank Creative Writing Group helps people develop their writing skills.

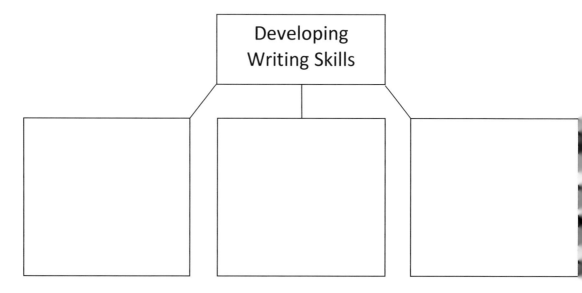

8   Read these sentences from the passage.

> **If you wish to unlock your creative skill for an exciting pastime, then we can help you. If you dream of being a published author, then we can help you make that happen.**

Why does the author most likely include these sentences?

Ⓐ   To warn the reader that the workshops may be difficult

Ⓑ   To excite the reader about what may be possible

Ⓒ   To suggest that the reader should have a clear goal

Ⓓ   To describe the successes of past students

9 Which word best describes the tone of the passage?

- Ⓐ Comforting
- Ⓑ Straightforward
- Ⓒ Encouraging
- Ⓓ Modest

10 Select the **two** sentences from paragraph 2 that best support the idea that the River Bank Creative Writing Group tailors programs to suit each individual. Tick **two** boxes below to show your choices.

- ☐ *We are based in Brooklyn, New York.*
- ☐ *We started our community organization in the fall of 2001.*
- ☐ *In the years since then, we have brought creative writing into the lives of many local residents.*
- ☐ *It does not matter whether you wish to write creatively as a hobby or as a way of making money.*
- ☐ *We have experienced and skilled staff to help you achieve success.*
- ☐ *We start by teaching the very basics of creative writing.*
- ☐ *Then we develop a program that is unique to your skills and goals.*
- ☐ *This can focus on writing short stories, poetry, plays, or anything else that interests you.*

A New Start

August 2, 2013

Dear Aunt Jamie,

What a day! I started at my new school this morning and had the best time. I made lots of new friends and really liked my teachers. I was so nervous the night before, but I had no reason to be. Everyone was so friendly and polite. They made me feel at ease. It was like I'd been at the school for a hundred years!

The day started very early at exactly 7 o'clock. I didn't want to feel rushed, so I made sure to get up early. I had my breakfast downstairs with my mom. She could tell that I was very anxious. Mom kept asking me what was wrong. I admitted that I was scared that people wouldn't like me or that everyone would just ignore me. She told me I had nothing to worry about and that everyone was going to love me. If they didn't love me, Mom said to send them her way for a good talking to. I couldn't stop laughing.

My mom dropped me off at the school gates about ten minutes before the bell. A little blond girl got dropped off at the same time and started waving at me. She ran over and told me her name was Abigail. She was very nice and we became close straight away. We spent all morning together and began to chat to another girl called Stacey. The three of us sat together in class all day and we even made our way home together! It went so quickly. Our teacher told us that tomorrow we would really start learning and developing new skills.

It is late now so I am going to sleep, but I cannot wait until tomorrow! I feel as though I am really going to enjoy my time at my new school. I only hope that my new friends feel the same way too.

Lots of love,

Casey

11   Which of these is the opening of the letter?

   Ⓐ   *A New Start*

   Ⓑ   *August 2, 2013*

   Ⓒ   *Dear Aunt Jamie,*

   Ⓓ   *Lots of love,*

12   Read this statement from the first paragraph of the letter.

   What a day!

   Circle the emotion that best describes what Casey uses this statement to show. Then explain how the details in the first paragraph helped you choose your answer.

   nervousness   excitement   surprise   relief

   _____

   _____

   _____

   _____

13   Read this sentence from the letter.

She was very nice and we became close straight away.

What does Casey mean when she says that they "became close"?

- Ⓐ   They began to be friends.
- Ⓑ   They walked near each other.
- Ⓒ   They stayed on their own.
- Ⓓ   They were in the same class.

14   What will Casey most likely do when she arrives at school the next day?

- Ⓐ   Sit by herself in the playground
- Ⓑ   See if there are any other new people
- Ⓒ   Look for Abigail and Stacey
- Ⓓ   Go to class early to see her teacher

15   Which word means the opposite of polite?

- Ⓐ   Rude
- Ⓑ   Nice
- Ⓒ   Easygoing
- Ⓓ   Calm

16 The reader can tell that Casey's mother –

- Ⓐ is used to meeting new people
- Ⓑ is very worried about her daughter
- Ⓒ cares about Casey's feelings
- Ⓓ wishes Casey did not have to start a new school

17 Based on your answer to Question 16, describe how Casey's mother's actions show what she is like.

_____

_____

_____

_____

_____

18 Which word would Casey most likely use to describe Abigail?

- Ⓐ Funny
- Ⓑ Friendly
- Ⓒ Bossy
- Ⓓ Shy

19 Casey writes that "It was like I'd been at the school for a hundred years!" What is this an example of?

- Ⓐ Imagery, using details to create an image or picture
- Ⓑ Hyperbole, using exaggeration to make a point
- Ⓒ Flashback, describing events that occurred far in the past
- Ⓓ Symbolism, using an object to stand for something else

20 Think about your answer to Question 19. What is the statement Casey makes used to show?

- Ⓐ How bored Casey is
- Ⓑ How comfortable Casey feels
- Ⓒ How there is too much new information to take in
- Ⓓ How the school has a long history

21 How is Casey's day different from what she expected? Use details from the passage to support your answer.

_____

_____

_____

_____

_____

_____

The Inventor

1) Scott had always been creative. Ever since he had been a child, he had loved to experiment with new ideas. As Scott had grown, his passion had only grown stronger. After attending university, Scott decided that he wanted to become an inventor. He used his studies in engineering to design and produce many brand new things. His friends thought that he was misguided.

2) "You cannot spend your life as an inventor," said his best friend Luke. "You will never have a steady income."

3) Luke worked as a bank manager and worried for his friend's future.

4) "Why don't you reconsider and get a job in the city?" Luke often asked. "You can always invent on the weekends."

5) But Scott would not be distracted from his goals.

6) "This is my dream," he said to Luke. "I have wanted to be an inventor since I was a small child. I am not going to give up."

7) "But you might spend years trying and never make it," Luke said. "You don't want to look back and realize you wasted all your time and talent. You're a great engineer, so you know you could get a good job somewhere and do well for yourself."

8) Scott would explain that he didn't want to work making things that had already been invented. There was no challenge in that. He wanted to use his talents to create something new that would improve how things were done.

9) Luke would shrug and leave his friend to his many different projects. Over several years, Scott developed many ideas that failed to become a success. His first invention was a device that was designed to make a car use less fuel as it traveled. This had many flaws and Scott was unable to sell his invention.

10) His second idea was a special motorcycle helmet that provided better vision for riders. This invention received little support from people who worked in the industry. Scott's friend Luke continued to encourage him to find a different career.

11) "Scott, you have to think about your future. I am proud of you for trying so hard to follow your dreams. I think it is now time to try something else. If you don't, I worry about how things will turn out for you."

12) "Thank you Luke," Scott replied. "I appreciate it. But I cannot stop now. I am so close to coming up with something huge. If I left my designs now, all my life would have been wasted."

13) Luke nodded, "I understand my friend. Just know that I am here to support you."

14) Then one day it happened. Scott completed his design of a new wing for an airplane. It had taken six months. Scott's new invention would improve the efficiency of the plane. He presented it to several companies who all loved his idea. After some competition, a company offered to buy his idea and design plans. Scott accepted the offer.

15) "I knew that one day I would make it!" he said to Luke as they celebrated at his apartment.

16) Luke felt a little guilty for ever suggesting that Scott should give up.

17) "I don't know how you kept going all these years," Luke said. "You definitely deserve every bit of your success."

22 In the sentence below, which word could best be used in place of flaws?

   This had many flaws and Scott was unable to sell his invention.

   Ⓐ Costs

   Ⓑ Faults

   Ⓒ Benefits

   Ⓓ Uses

23 Read this sentence from the passage.

   As Scott had grown, his passion had only grown stronger.

   The word passion shows that Scott is very –

   Ⓐ enthusiastic

   Ⓑ talented

   Ⓒ impatient

   Ⓓ knowledgeable

24 Which statement best describes how the photograph at the start of the passage relates to the information in the first paragraph?

   Ⓐ It shows how Scott loved to experiment with new ideas.

   Ⓑ It shows how Scott's passion increased as he got older.

   Ⓒ It shows how Scott studied engineering at university.

   Ⓓ It shows how Scott's goals were misguided.

25 According to the passage, what did Scott study at college?

- Ⓐ Science
- Ⓑ Mathematics
- Ⓒ Engineering
- Ⓓ Aviation

26 What type of passage is "The Inventor"?

- Ⓐ Realistic fiction
- Ⓑ Science fiction
- Ⓒ Biography
- Ⓓ Fable

27 Complete the table below by listing **two** reasons that Scott gives for continuing to chase his dream of being an inventor and **two** reasons that Luke gives for getting a regular job.

Scott's Reasons for Being an Inventor	Luke's Reasons for Getting a Regular Job

28   The main theme of the passage is about –

   Ⓐ   not giving up on your dreams

   Ⓑ   making the world a better place

   Ⓒ   improving on old ideas

   Ⓓ   making time for your friends

29   Based on your answer to Question 28, choose **two** paragraphs that support your answer. On the lines below, explain how each paragraph supports your answer.

   Paragraph: _____

   _____

   _____

   _____

   _____

   Paragraph: _____

   _____

   _____

   _____

   _____

30 Which word best describes Scott?

- Ⓐ Foolish
- Ⓑ Determined
- Ⓒ Easygoing
- Ⓓ Sensible

31 Based on your answer to Question 30, give **two** details from the passage that support your answer.

1: _____

_____

2: _____

_____

32 Circle **all** the words from the passage that contain prefixes.

creative	experiment	passion	stronger
university	misguided	reconsider	talent
projects	challenge	improve	different
unable	understand	competition	success

33 The table below describes Scott's inventions and their benefits. Complete the table using details from the passage.

Scott's Inventions

Invention	Benefit of the Invention
Device for a car	Reduced the amount of fuel used
Motorcycle helmet	
New airplane wing	

END OF PRACTICE TEST

SOL Reading

Practice Test 3

Instructions

Read each passage and answer the questions that follow it.

For each multiple-choice question, fill in the circle for the correct answer. For other types of questions, follow the instructions given. Some of the questions require a written answer. Write your answer on the lines provided.

Mark Zuckerberg

Mark Zuckerberg is a web site developer and computer programmer. He is also a businessperson. He is best known for creating the web site Facebook. Facebook is a web site that allows people to connect with friends and family. He is now the CEO and president of the company.

Zuckerberg founded the web site in 2004 with some of his Harvard University classmates. He has since overseen the development of the site. Facebook became the most visited online web site throughout 2010. This was also the year that Mark Zuckerberg was named as Person of the Year by *Time Magazine*.

Mark Zuckerberg was born in White Plains, New York in 1984. His early education was spent at Ardsley High School. This was followed by Phillips Exeter Academy. While at Phillips Exeter Academy, he won prizes for his work in science, mathematics, astronomy, and physics. His outdoor pursuits included fencing, and he was captain of the college fencing team. He is also multilingual and can speak French, Latin, Hebrew, and Ancient Greek.

Zuckerberg first showed an interest in computers during middle school. At this time, he started to write software programs. His father hired an experienced software developer, David Newman, to tutor his son. He was identified at this young age to be an amazing talent. This encouraged him to take a graduate course in software design while at high school. He continued to develop computer programs as he learned.

Zuckerberg's main interest was in software that helped people to interact and communicate. This passion inspired a program called ZuckNet. This allowed a small set of users to communicate by 'pinging' each other. It was like a basic version of today's instant messenger tools. Zuckerberg continued to experiment with different software programs. Then he enrolled at Harvard University. During this time, he focused on creating software that connected people through common interests. The inspiration for Facebook came from paper-based books at the university. The books were known as facebooks and showed students' names, photographs, and gave information about them.

Facebook was launched on February 4, 2004. At first it was only for Harvard University students. It soon spread to other major universities including Stanford, Columbia, Yale, and MIT. This was followed by a spread to most universities in the United States. In 2005, it was made available to high schools. This was followed by allowing people from large companies like Apple and Microsoft to join. In 2006, it was made available to anyone over the age of 13. The site has grown rapidly since then. In 2012, Facebook had over one billion users worldwide.

On May 18, 2012, Facebook took another major step in its history. It listed on the stock exchange. It was one of the biggest listings in history. On the day of its listing, Facebook had a total value of just over $100 billion. Mark Zuckerberg was given the honor of ringing the bell to open stock market trading on the day. He rang the bell from the Facebook campus in California surrounded by cheering staff.

The site continues to grow and change. As of January 2014, Zuckerberg remains as chairman and CEO of Facebook, and has an estimated total wealth of just over $25 billion. In 2010, he pledged to give at least half of his wealth to charity over his lifetime. His donations have included giving over $100 million to public schools in New Jersey, supporting various small Internet businesses, and giving almost $1 billion worth of Facebook shares to the Silicon Valley Community Foundation.

One other thing Mark Zuckerberg is known for is wearing hoodies. While a suit and tie is the expected choice for a business meeting, he appears at many wearing a hoodie and slide-on sandals. This kind of casual clothing is also usually his choice for presentations and other public events. Some have said that his style of dress shows his lack of seriousness. Others argue that he values what he does above what he looks like.

© Elaine Chan and Priscilla Chan, Wikimedia Commons

1 As it is used in the sentence, what does the word <u>common</u> mean?

> **During this time, he focused on creating software that connected people through common interests.**

- Ⓐ Ordinary
- Ⓑ Everyday
- Ⓒ Shared
- Ⓓ General

2 Read this sentence from the passage.

> **He is also multilingual and can speak French, Latin, Hebrew, and Ancient Greek.**

What does the prefix in the word <u>multilingual</u> mean? Explain how the sentence helps show the meaning of the prefix.

_____

_____

_____

_____

_____

3   Place the following groups in order from first to gain access to Facebook to last to gain access to Facebook. Write the numbers 1, 2, 3, and 4 on the lines to show the order.

___ Students of major universities

___ Employees of large companies

___ High school students

___ Harvard University students

4   Which paragraph has the main purpose of describing how Zuckerberg first developed his computer skills? Circle the paragraph you have selected.

Paragraph 1   Paragraph 2   Paragraph 3   Paragraph 4

Paragraph 5   Paragraph 6   Paragraph 7   Paragraph 8

5   Which sentence from the passage best shows that Facebook is successful?
- Ⓐ   *Facebook is a web site that allows people to connect with friends and family.*
- Ⓑ   *Facebook became the most visited online web site throughout 2010.*
- Ⓒ   *Facebook was launched on February 4, 2004.*
- Ⓓ   *This was followed by allowing people from large companies like Apple and Microsoft to join.*

6   Why did Mark Zuckerberg's father most likely hire a software developer to tutor his son?

    Ⓐ   He was worried that Mark was making mistakes.

    Ⓑ   He saw that Mark had a talent worth developing.

    Ⓒ   He saw that Mark was struggling with his studies.

    Ⓓ   He wanted Mark to develop useful programs.

7   This passage is most like –

    Ⓐ   a biography

    Ⓑ   an autobiography

    Ⓒ   a short story

    Ⓓ   a news article

8   In paragraph 3, the author describes how Zuckerberg won prizes for his work in several areas, was captain of the fencing team, and is multilingual. Explain why you think the author chose to include these details.

    _____

    _____

    _____

    _____

    _____

9   The web below summarizes information from the passage.

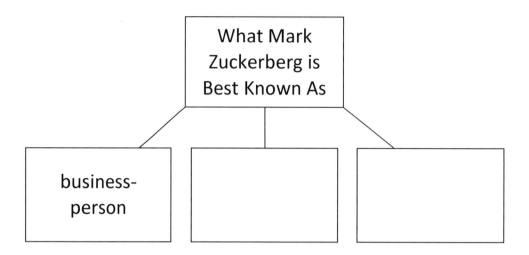

Complete the web by choosing the **two** best options from those given below. Write your answers in the web.

| teacher | fencing champion | computer programmer |

| web site developer | author | college professor |

10   The passage describes how successful Mark Zuckerberg has become. Describe **one** lesson about becoming successful people can learn from the passage. Use details from the passage in your answer.

_____

_____

_____

_____

_____

_____

11   What does the photograph and the caption show about Zuckerberg's personality? Explain your answer.

_____

_____

_____

_____

_____

_____

The Aspiring Star

Troy longed to be a professional basketball player. He had loved the sport ever since he was a small child. He was also very skilled and fast on the basketball court. Despite this, he had one small problem. He was very short. His school coach had suggested that he would never make it in the professional leagues. Although he was devastated at first, he refused to give up on his dream.

Troy had several trials at professional clubs but failed to earn a contract. It was then that he attended the training ground of the Los Angeles Lakers. He asked the coach for a trial. As usual, he was refused. It wasn't in his nature just to walk away.

"But you haven't even given me a chance," said Troy.

"Why should I give you a shot?" asked the coach.

Troy paused before he answered.

"Because one day I am going to be the best player in the world and I will be able to help you out," he replied seriously.

The coach smiled at the confidence of the answer.

"Alright kid," he said. "I'll give you a chance to impress me."

Troy took part in a short practice match and was then allowed to showcase his individual skills. He knew he was being given a rare chance and he put everything he had into it. While the other players took a break for water, Troy stayed on the court and showed even more of his ball skills. He was one of the most skillful players on show and had the will to win to match. The coach was stunned.

"You certainly have a lot of talent for a little fellow," he said. "How would you like to sign on a youth contract?"

Troy agreed and was soon rising through the ranks. He was the shortest player by far, but he was also the hardest worker. He felt he had to work hard to overcome the natural height that he lacked. He practiced his ball skills far longer than everyone else. While he couldn't leap as high as everyone else, he was fast and could dribble the ball around everyone. It was rare to see Troy lose the ball or have it stolen from him. He often stole it from other players, and especially those who underestimated him.

Although some players continued to think he was too short to play, they soon changed their minds when they saw him in action. After two short years, he was a regular for the Lakers and had even won the award as the team's most valuable player. Even with Troy's help, the team was struggling. They were not winning many games and there were rumors that the coach was close to losing his job. It was before a game against the New York Jets that he called Troy into his office for a discussion.

"I have heard that if we lose tonight then I will be replaced as coach," he told Troy. "I need you to do more than play well tonight. I need you to carry the team and win the game. Do you remember your promise before I signed you?"

Troy nodded and smiled at his coach.

"You bet I do coach," he replied. "You bet I do."

Troy went on to play the game of his life that evening. The Lakers won the game and won every game that was left that season. The coach kept his job and led his team on to success.

12 Read this sentence from the passage.

> **Although he was devastated at first, he refused to give up on his dream.**

The word <u>devastated</u> means that Troy was –

- Ⓐ understanding
- Ⓑ very upset
- Ⓒ not surprised
- Ⓓ slightly amused

13 Read this sentence from the passage.

> **I need you to carry the team and win the game.**

What does the phrase "carry the team" refer to?

- Ⓐ How Troy will have to cheer on his teammates
- Ⓑ How Troy will have to do extra work
- Ⓒ How Troy will have to motivate the team
- Ⓓ How Troy will have to go against his team

14 What is the main hurdle that makes it difficult for Troy to play at a high level? How does Troy make up for it?

_____

_____

_____

_____

_____

15 Which statement best describes the theme of the passage?

- Ⓐ It is important to keep your promises.
- Ⓑ You can achieve your dreams if you work hard enough.
- Ⓒ Confidence is the key to being great.
- Ⓓ There is no time like the present.

16 In the third paragraph, Troy asks to be given a chance. How does this affect the rest of the events?

- Ⓐ It proves to the coach that Troy is fearless enough to do well.
- Ⓑ It helps Troy understand what it will take to achieve his goal.
- Ⓒ It encourages the coach to be more open-minded about players.
- Ⓓ It allows the coach to see how talented Troy is and get a contract.

17 Read this sentence from the end of the passage spoken by the coach.

Do you remember your promise before I signed you?

What promise is the coach referring to? Explain your answer.

_____

_____

_____

_____

_____

18 What is the point of view in the passage?

Ⓐ First person

Ⓑ Second person

Ⓒ Third person limited

Ⓓ Third person omniscient

19 How do you think the coach feels about his decision to give Troy a chance at the end of the passage? Use details from the passage to support your answer.

20 Troy's story can be described as inspiring. Explain why Troy's story is inspiring. Use details from the passage in your answer.

21 Complete the web below by listing **three** ways Troy's height actually helped him.

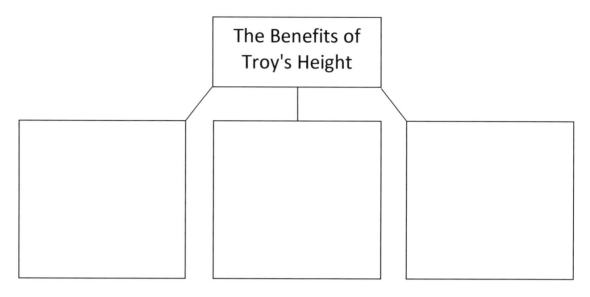

22 Describe **two** examples from the passage that show how Troy takes advantage of every chance he is given.

1: _____

_____

2: _____

_____

Spinning the Spider's Web

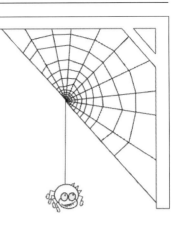

The spider spins his silken web,
In the corner of my home,
He weaves it for his family,
One teeny space their own.

I watch him as he toils,
Through the hours of the day,
Spinning as the summer burns,
Forever building come what may.

And when his web is broken,
He never sheds a tear,
He simply spins and starts again,
And keeps his loved ones near.

This small kingdom is his castle,
And a tiny place to rest,
Although some may beg to differ,
He builds his home to be the best.

He goes about his business,
And does not seek to pry or scare,
He means no harm to those around him,
To cross your path, he wouldn't dare.

The spider just keeps on spinning,
His winding, silken web,
Building homes amongst the darkness,
Keeping family in good stead.

So next time you see the spider,
Spinning webs inside your home,
Think how hard he has to toil,
Without a single word or moan.

23 Read this line from the poem.

I watch him as he toils,

What does the word toils mean?

- Ⓐ Works
- Ⓑ Spins
- Ⓒ Struggles
- Ⓓ Plays

24 Read this line from the poem.

One teeny space their own.

Complete the chart by dividing the words listed below into synonyms of teeny and antonyms of teeny.

tiny   giant   small   massive

little   huge   great   minute

Synonyms	Antonyms

25 What does the poet seem to find most impressive about spiders?

   Ⓐ That they can live anywhere

   Ⓑ That they never stop working

   Ⓒ That they are not afraid of anything

   Ⓓ That they leave people alone

26 Think about your answer to Question 25. Write **two** lines below that support your answer to Question 25. Explain what each line shows about the poet's opinion of spiders.

   Line 1: _____

   _____

   _____

   Line 2: _____

   _____

   _____

27 Which stanza of the poem has a message about facing disappointments?

   Ⓐ Stanza 1

   Ⓑ Stanza 2

   Ⓒ Stanza 3

   Ⓓ Stanza 4

28 Based on your answer to Question 27, explain how the poet communicates the message about overcoming disappointments.

_____

_____

_____

_____

_____

29 Which literary technique does the poet use in the first line of the poem?

- Ⓐ Alliteration
- Ⓑ Simile
- Ⓒ Metaphor
- Ⓓ Flashback

30 What is the rhyme pattern of each stanza of the poem?

- Ⓐ All the lines rhyme with each other.
- Ⓑ There are two pairs of rhyming lines.
- Ⓒ The second and fourth lines rhyme.
- Ⓓ None of the lines rhyme.

31 Which statement would the poet most likely agree with?

- Ⓐ People should make their own homes like spiders do.
- Ⓑ People should keep their homes free from spider webs.
- Ⓒ People should be aware of the dangers of spiders.
- Ⓓ People should leave spiders alone.

32 The poet states that "to cross your path, he wouldn't dare." What does the phrase "cross your path" refer to?

- Ⓐ Scaring someone
- Ⓑ Running into someone
- Ⓒ Stealing from someone
- Ⓓ Arguing with someone

33 Describe what people can learn from the spider about hard work and determination.

_____

_____

_____

_____

END OF PRACTICE TEST

ANSWER KEY

Virginia's New State Standards

In 2017, the state of Virginia adopted new *Standards of Learning*. The *Standards of Learning* describe what students are expected to know. All the exercises and questions in this book cover the *Standards of Learning* introduced in 2017.

Reading Standards and Reporting Categories

The reading standards are divided into the following areas:

- Use word analysis strategies and word reference materials
- Demonstrate comprehension of fictional texts
- Demonstrate comprehension of nonfiction texts

Within each of these areas, there are standards that describe specific skills the student should have. The answer key that follows lists the standard assessed by each question.

Scoring Written Answer Questions

This workbook includes written answer questions. The answer key gives guidance on how to score these questions. Use the criteria listed as a guide to scoring these questions, and as a guide for giving the student advice on how to improve an answer.

SOL Reading, Mini-Test 1

Question	Answer	SOL Reading Standard
1	B	Use context to clarify meaning of unfamiliar words and phrases.
2	D	Use knowledge of roots, affixes, synonyms, antonyms, and homophones to determine the meaning of new words.
3	B	Describe character development.
4	See Below	Summarize plot events using details from text.
5	B	Identify an author's use of figurative language.
6	B	Identify genres.
7	See Below	Draw conclusions and make inferences with support from the text.
8	C	Draw conclusions and make inferences with support from the text.
9	C	Identify theme(s).
10	See Below	Identify cause and effect relationships.
11	See Below	Explain the resolution of conflict(s).
12	See Below	Summarize plot events using details from text.
13	A	Use context to clarify meaning of unfamiliar words and phrases.
14	help, assistance	Use knowledge of roots, affixes, synonyms, antonyms, and homophones to determine the meaning of new words.
15	D	Differentiate between fact and opinion.
16	C	Identify the main idea.
17	D	Identify the main idea.
18	See Below	Summarize supporting details.
19	C	Locate information from the text to support opinions, inferences, and conclusions.
20	See Below	Locate information from the text to support opinions, inferences, and conclusions.
21	B	Identify cause and effect relationships.
22	1st, 2nd, 4th, and 6th	Identify cause and effect relationships.
23	See Below	Locate information from the text to support opinions, inferences, and conclusions.
24	She makes class fun. She explains things clearly.	Summarize supporting details.
25	C	Identify organizational pattern(s).

Q4.
Give a score of 0, 1, or 2 based on how well the answer meets the criteria listed below.
- It should give a reasonable explanation of why Tara has mixed feelings about the trip.
- The answer should show an understanding that she is excited about the trip, but scared because she has to fly.

Q7.
Give a score of 0, 1, or 2 based on how well the answer meets the criteria listed below.
- It should explain that Tara's father had a similar experience with a fear he had when he was young.
- It may refer to how Tara's father understands how she feels or understands how she can overcome the fear.

Q10.
Give a score of 1 for each correct cause and effect relationship described. A sample answer is given below.
- Tara is afraid of flying. / Tara doesn't want to go on a trip to New Zealand.
- Tara's father was afraid of spiders. / Tara's father did not want to go camping.

Q11.
Give a score of 0, 1, or 2 based on how well the answer meets the criteria listed below.
- The student should give a reasonable explanation of what Tara means by saying that she is going whether her fear likes it or not. The answer should refer to how she has decided not to give in to fear or not to let fear control her.

Q12.
Give a score of 0, 1, or 2 based on how well the answer meets the criteria listed below.
- It should explain that Tara wanting to do the things in New Zealand makes her braver because it motivates her to overcome her fears. The answer may also refer to how she is going to focus on doing the fun things instead of worrying about her fear.

Q18.
Give a score of 0, 1, or 2 based on how many correct supporting details are given.
- The answer may refer to how Miss Hooper made every subject fun and interesting, never made Jacob feel silly for asking a question, or explained things several times if she needed to.

Q20.
Give a score of 0, 1, or 2 based on how well the answer meets the criteria listed below.
- The student should explain how you can tell that Jacob is sad about losing Miss Hooper but understanding.
- The answer may refer to his "mixed feelings," to how he is sad about losing her, to how he is glad she will be able to help others, or to how he says it would be selfish to keep her all through school.

Q23.
Give a score of 0, 1, or 2 based on how well the answer meets the criteria listed below.
- It should explain why starting a new school turned out to be a huge blessing for Jacob.
- It should refer to the influence Miss Hooper had on Jacob and how it has changed how he feels about school.

SOL Reading, Mini-Test 2

Question	Answer	SOL Reading Standard
1	D	Use context to clarify meaning of unfamiliar words and phrases.
2	B	Identify organizational pattern(s).
3	Making a Choice	Use text features such as type, headings, and graphics, to predict and categorize information.
4	B	Use knowledge of roots, affixes, synonyms, antonyms, and homophones to determine the meaning of new words.
5	See Below	Locate information from the text to support opinions, inferences, and conclusions.
6	Watch videos online / Visit web sites	Skim materials to develop a general overview of content and to locate specific information.
7	A	Identify the main idea.
8	C	Locate information from the text to support opinions, inferences, and conclusions.
9	A	Locate information from the text to support opinions, inferences, and conclusions.
10	B	Use text features such as type, headings, and graphics, to predict and categorize information.
11	See Below	Summarize supporting details.
12	C	Use text features such as type, headings, and graphics, to predict and categorize information.
13	See Below	Skim materials to develop a general overview of content and to locate specific information.
14	B	Use context and sentence structure to determine meanings and differentiate among multiple meanings of words.
15	D	Explain how an author's choice of vocabulary contributes to the author's style.
16	A	Summarize plot events using details from text.
17	B	Identify theme(s).
18	See Below	Explain the resolution of conflict(s).
19	B	Summarize plot events using details from text.
20	A	Draw conclusions and make inferences with support from the text.
21	See Below	Summarize plot events using details from text.
22	C	Describe character development.
23	D	Identify cause and effect relationships.
24	See Below	Identify cause and effect relationships.
25	See Below	Explain the resolution of conflict(s).

Q5.
Give a score of 0, 1, or 2 based on how well the answer meets the criteria listed below.
- It should give at least two plausible reasons that tell why choosing an instrument is such an important step.
- The answer may refer to not wasting money on the wrong instrument, to being sure to choose an instrument that suits how you want to play it, or to choosing an instrument that you will be able to learn.

Q11.
Give a score of 0, 1, 2, or 3 based on how many ways from the passage are listed. A sample answer is given below.
- Borrow it from a friend or relative. / Borrow it from your school. / Buy a secondhand instrument.

Q13.
Give a score of 0.5 for each correct pair of instruments listed. A sample answer is given below.
- Orchestra: flute / saxophone   Marching band: trumpet / trombone
- Playing and singing: piano / guitar   Rock band: guitar / drums

Q18.
Give a score of 0, 1, or 2 based on how well the answer meets the criteria listed below.
- It should give a reasonable summary of how the outcome for the wasps teaches a lesson about being honest.
- The answer should show an understanding that the wasps lied and were caught lying.

Q21.
Give a score of 0, 1, or 2 based on how well the answer meets the criteria listed below.
- It should give a reasonable explanation of how the wasps panicking affects the judge.
- The answer should refer to how the judge realizes that the wasps must not be able to make honey.

Q24.
Give a score of 0.5 for each correct similarity or difference and for each correct effect listed. A sample answer is given below.
- Similarity: The bees and wasps have yellow and black striped bodies. / Nobody can be sure whether it was the bees or the wasps near the tree.
- Difference: Only the bees can make honey. / The wasps panic when they are asked to make honey.

Q25.
Give a score of 0, 1, or 2 based on how well the answer meets the criteria listed below.
- It should describe the main problem as being that nobody can tell whether the honey belongs to the wasps or the bees.
- It should clearly explain how the problem is resolved. This should refer to how the judge tells the wasps and bees to make honey, and realizes by how the wasps respond that they are unable to make honey.

SOL Reading, Mini-Test 3

Question	Answer	SOL Reading Standard
1	creepy ghostly scary	Use knowledge of roots, affixes, synonyms, antonyms, and homophones to determine the meaning of new words.
2	6th, 7th, and 10th	Discuss the impact of setting on plot development.
3	B	Explain how an author's choice of vocabulary contributes to the author's style.
4	See Below	Explain how an author's choice of vocabulary contributes to the author's style.
5	B	Draw conclusions and make inferences with support from the text.
6	A	Identify an author's use of figurative language.
7	B	Identify cause and effect relationships.
8	See Below	Draw conclusions and make inferences with support from the text.
9	D	Differentiate between first and third person point-of-view.
10	A	Compare/contrast details in literary and informational nonfiction texts.
11	B	Describe character development.
12	See Below	Draw conclusions and make inferences with support from the text.
13	See Below	Discuss the impact of setting on plot development.
14	A	Use word-reference materials.
15	D	Differentiate between fact and opinion.
16	See Below	Summarize supporting details.
17	A	Skim materials to develop a general overview of content and to locate specific information.
18	See Below	Identify organizational pattern(s).
19	famous, well-known	Use knowledge of roots, affixes, synonyms, antonyms, and homophones to determine the meaning of new words.
20	A	Compare and contrast details and ideas within and between texts.
21	F, F, F, O	Differentiate between fact and opinion.
22	See Below	Summarize supporting details.
23	B	Compare and contrast details and ideas within and between texts.
24	B	Identify the main idea.
25	A	Use word-reference materials.

Q4.
Give a score of 0, 1, or 2 based on how well the answer meets the criteria listed below.
- It should give a reasonable explanation of how Rick feels based on how he edges toward the door.
- The student should describe how he feels scared, nervous, or uncertain.

Q8.
Give a score of 0, 1, or 2 based on how many relevant details are given.
- Any detail from the passage that shows Rick's fear can be accepted.
- The student may describe how he is quiet on the way to the lighthouse, how he tells Simon to go first, how he is not keen to open the door, or how he shouts and runs away when he hears a noise.

Q12.
Give a score of 0, 1, or 2 based on how well the answer meets the criteria listed below.
- The student should circle one of the words and provide an explanation to support the choice.
- Either answer is acceptable as long as the student explains it and supports it with relevant details.
- The student could argue that Simon is cowardly for being afraid or that Simon is brave for facing his fear.

Q13.
Give a score of 0.5 for each correct factual detail or personal opinion given. A sample answer is given below.
- Factual Details: It is two miles from Simon's house. / It is two hundred years old. / It casts a light for miles.
- Simon's Opinions or Feelings: It is haunted. / It is eerie. / It looks like a ghost at night.

Q16.
Give a score of 1 for each row of the table correctly completed. The correct answers are given below.
- Brazil 5 / Italy 4 / Germany 3

Q18.
Give a score of 0.5 for each sentence correctly matched. The correct answers are given below.
- The 2013 championship... – a fact given to support a claim
- This is much less than for... – a comparison
- However, soccer is a very... – an opinion
- Soccer may become a... – a prediction

Q22.
Give a score of 0, 1, or 2 based on how many correct supporting details are given.
- The details may include that the team has won the English Premier League nineteen times, that the team has won the English Premier League more times than any other team, and that the team has won the European Champions League three times.

SOL Reading, Practice Test 1

Question	Answer	SOL Reading Standard
1	A	Explain how an author's choice of vocabulary contributes to the author's style.
2	B	Use knowledge of roots, affixes, synonyms, antonyms, and homophones to determine the meaning of new words.
3	C	Draw conclusions and make inferences with support from the text.
4	B	Identify an author's use of figurative language.
5	D	Draw conclusions and make inferences with support from the text.
6	special and unforgettable	Describe character development.
7	See Below	Discuss the impact of setting on plot development.
8	See Below	Describe character development.
9	See Below	Draw conclusions and make inferences with support from the text.
10	See Below	Explain how an author's choice of vocabulary contributes to the author's style.
11	B	Use context to clarify meaning of unfamiliar words and phrases.
12	See Below	Skim materials to develop a general overview of content and to locate specific information.
13	B	Use word-reference materials.
14	D	Identify transitional words and phrases that signal an author's organizational pattern.
15	A	Identify the main idea.
16	B	Use text features such as type, headings, and graphics, to predict and categorize information.
17	Step 4	Skim materials to develop a general overview of content and to locate specific information.
18	See Below	Locate information from the text to support opinions, inferences, and conclusions.
19	D	Identify organizational pattern(s).
20	See Below	Summarize supporting details.
21	C	Identify an author's use of figurative language.
22	See Below	Identify an author's use of figurative language.
23	A	Draw conclusions and make inferences with support from the text.
24	A	Differentiate between free verse and rhymed poetry.
25	1st and 5th	Identify an author's use of figurative language.
26	C	Explain how an author's choice of vocabulary contributes to the author's style.
27	B	Draw conclusions and make inferences with support from the text.
28	B	Describe character development.
29	Stanza 5	Compare/contrast details in literary and informational nonfiction texts.
30	See Below	Compare/contrast details in literary and informational nonfiction texts.
31	B	Explain how an author's choice of vocabulary contributes to the author's style.
32	See Below	Discuss the impact of setting on plot development.
33	See Below	Summarize plot events using details from text.

Q7.
Give a score of 0, 1, or 2 based on how well the answer meets the criteria listed below.
- The student should identify that paragraph 2 contains a flashback.
- It should describe how the flashback tells how Emma first felt when she learned she was going to have a brother.

Q8.
Give a score of 0, 1, or 2 based on how well the answer meets the criteria listed below.
- It should give details that show that Emma is excited about having a baby brother.
- The details may include that she cannot sleep the night before, that she cannot concentrate on anything while waiting to go to the hospital, that she feels like the trip to the hospital takes a long time, or that she can't stop smiling when she sees her brother.

Q9.
Give a score of 0, 1, or 2 based on how many relevant details are given.
- The details may include that she does not smile, that she worries about him crying all the time, that she worries about losing her room, or that she thinks her mother might not come to her dance competitions.

Q10.
Give a score of 1 for each phrase added that creates a sense of calm.
- The phrases could include any of the following: took him in my arms; cradled his tiny little baby body; slowly opened his eyes; gazed up at me; deepest blue; smile softly; slowly closed his eyes; or drifted off to sleep.

Q12.
Give a score of 0, 1, or 2 based on how well the answer meets the criteria listed below.
- The student should circle two steps and provide a reasonable description of how those steps would create a polished story. The most likely steps to be circled are 5, 6, or 8.
- The answer must describe how the two steps would create a polished story.

Q18.
Give a score of 0, 1, or 2 based on how well the answer meets the criteria listed below.
- It should identify that the protagonist is the hero of the story and the antagonist is the villain of the story.
- It should give a reasonable explanation of why having both would keep the story interesting, such as by explaining that the reader would want the hero to overcome the villain.

Q20.
Give a score of 0, 1, or 2 based on how well the answer meets the criteria listed below.
- It should identify details that show that writing a good story is not easy.
- The details may include that it takes many steps to write a good story, that many things need to be considered when writing a story, or that a good story needs to be checked and revised.

Q22.
Give a score of 0, 1, or 2 based on how well the answer meets the criteria listed below.
- It should give a reasonable analysis of how the personification helps readers connect with the poem.
- It may refer to how readers understand the lily, understand the lily's feelings, or feel pleased that the lily feels good.

Q30.
Give a score of 0, 1, or 2 based on how well the answer meets the criteria listed below.
- It should identify that the lily feels upset, needy, or impatient in both stanzas 1 and 5.
- It should identify that the lily wants sunshine in the first stanza and rain in the fifth stanza.

Q32.
Give a score of 0, 1, or 2 based on how well the answer meets the criteria listed below.
- It should describe how the lines describe the lily collecting water when it rains.
- It should explain that the water cannot be collected until the sunshine makes the lily's petals stand upright.

Q33.
Give a score of 1 for each stanza identified that includes a reasonable explanation of what the dialogue tells the reader.
- The student may identify stanzas 3, 7, or 8.
- The explanation for each stanza may describe how the lily feels or why the lily feels that way.

SOL Reading, Practice Test 2

Question	Answer	SOL Reading Standard
1	C	Use context and sentence structure to determine meanings and differentiate among multiple meanings of words.
2	B	Identify the main idea.
3	See Below	Summarize supporting details.
4	B	Use text features such as type, headings, and graphics, to predict and categorize information.
5	C	Locate information from the text to support opinions, inferences, and conclusions.
6	A	Identify the main idea.
7	See Below	Summarize supporting details.
8	B	Compare and contrast details and ideas within and between texts.
9	C	Skim materials to develop a general overview of content and to locate specific information.
10	4th, 7th, or 8th	Locate information from the text to support opinions, inferences, and conclusions.
11	C	Compare/contrast details in literary and informational nonfiction texts.
12	See Below	Describe character development.
13	A	Use context and sentence structure to determine meanings and differentiate among multiple meanings of words.
14	C	Draw conclusions and make inferences with support from the text.
15	A	Use knowledge of roots, affixes, synonyms, antonyms, and homophones to determine the meaning of new words.
16	C	Describe character development.
17	See Below	Describe character development.
18	B	Draw conclusions and make inferences with support from the text.
19	B	Identify an author's use of figurative language.
20	B	Identify an author's use of figurative language.
21	See Below	Summarize plot events using details from text.
22	B	Use knowledge of roots, affixes, synonyms, antonyms, and homophones to determine the meaning of new words.
23	A	Use context to clarify meaning of unfamiliar words and phrases.
24	A	Compare/contrast details in literary and informational nonfiction texts.
25	C	Summarize plot events using details from text.
26	A	Identify genres.
27	See Below	Identify cause and effect relationships.
28	A	Identify theme(s).
29	See Below	Identify theme(s).
30	B	Describe character development.
31	See Below	Describe character development.
32	misguided reconsider unable	Use knowledge of roots, affixes, synonyms, antonyms, and homophones to determine the meaning of new words.
33	See Below	Summarize plot events using details from text.

Q3.
Give a score of 0, 1, or 2 based on how many correct supporting details are given.
- The supporting details given should be those that show the success of the writing group.
- The answer may refer to the student getting her novel published and becoming known worldwide, to the student having a poetry collection published, or to the thousands of skilled creative writers produced.

Q7.
Give a score of 1 for each correct way of developing writing skills listed. A sample answer is given below.
- Teaches the basics of creative writing. / Gives writers feedback. / Has guest speakers give advice.

Q12.
Give a score of 0, 1, or 2 based on how well the answer meets the criteria listed below.
- The student may circle excitement, surprise, or relief.
- The answer should include an analysis of how you can tell how Casey feels based on paragraph 1.

Q17.
Give a score of 0, 1, or 2 based on how well the answer meets the criteria listed below.
- It should describe how the mother's actions show that she cares about Casey's feelings.
- The answer may refer to how the mother keeps asking Casey what is wrong, how the mother knows that Casey is anxious, or how the mother gives Casey advice and tries to help her.

Q21.
Give a score of 0, 1, or 2 based on how well the answer meets the criteria listed below.
- It should compare how Casey expects the day to be with how it turns out.
- The answer should refer to how Casey worries about being ignored or not being liked, but finds everyone friendly and makes new friends easily.

Q27.
Give a score of 0.5 for each correct reason listed in the table. A sample answer is given below.
- Scott's Reasons: Being an inventor has always been his dream. / He want to improve how things are done.
- Luke's Reasons: He should get a regular income. / He might waste all his talent.

Q29.
Give a score of 1 for each paragraph that includes a reasonable explanation supporting the choice.
- The explanation for each paragraph should describe how it relates to the theme of not giving up on your dreams.

Q31.
Give a score of 0, 1, or 2 based on how many correct supporting details are given.
- The answer may refer to how he keeps going when his inventions fail, how he does not let Luke's concerns stop him, or how he says that he cannot stop.

Q33.
Give a score of 1 for each correct benefit listed in the table. A sample answer is given below.
- Motorcycle helmet: Improved rider vision   New airplane wing: Improved efficiency

SOL Reading, Practice Test 3

Question	Answer	SOL Reading Standard
1	C	Use context to clarify meaning of unfamiliar words and phrases.
2	See Below	Use knowledge of roots, affixes, synonyms, antonyms, and homophones to determine the meaning of new words.
3	2, 4, 3, 1	Skim materials to develop a general overview of content and to locate specific information.
4	Paragraph 4	Identify the main idea.
5	B	Summarize supporting details.
6	B	Identify cause and effect relationships.
7	A	Use text features such as type, headings, and graphics, to predict and categorize information.
8	See Below	Locate information from the text to support opinions, inferences, and conclusions.
9	See Below	Summarize supporting details.
10	See Below	Identify the main idea.
11	See Below	Use text features such as type, headings, and graphics, to predict and categorize information.
12	B	Use context to clarify meaning of unfamiliar words and phrases.
13	B	Use context and sentence structure to determine meanings and differentiate among multiple meanings of words.
14	See Below	Summarize plot events using details from text.
15	B	Identify theme(s).
16	D	Identify cause and effect relationships.
17	See Below	Summarize plot events using details from text.
18	D	Differentiate between first and third person point-of-view.
19	See Below	Describe character development.
20	See Below	Explain the resolution of conflict(s).
21	See Below	Summarize plot events using details from text.
22	See Below	Draw conclusions and make inferences with support from the text.
23	A	Use context to clarify meaning of unfamiliar words and phrases.
24	See Below	Use knowledge of roots, affixes, synonyms, antonyms, and homophones to determine the meaning of new words.
25	B	Draw conclusions and make inferences with support from the text.
26	See Below	Draw conclusions and make inferences with support from the text.
27	C	Compare/contrast details in literary and informational nonfiction texts.
28	See Below	Identify theme(s).
29	A	Identify an author's use of figurative language.
30	C	Differentiate between free verse and rhymed poetry.
31	D	Draw conclusions and make inferences with support from the text.
32	B	Use context and sentence structure to determine meanings and differentiate among multiple meanings of words.
33	See Below	Identify theme(s).

Q2.
Give a score of 0, 1, or 2 based on how well the answer meets the criteria listed below.
- The answer should identify that the prefix *multi* means many or more than one.
- The student should explain how you can tell the meaning by referring to the languages listed.

Q8.
Give a score of 0, 1, or 2 based on how well the answer meets the criteria listed below.
- It should give a reasonable explanation of why the author includes these details.
- The student may infer that the details are included to show Mark's talent, intelligence, or determination.

Q9.
Give a score of 1 for each correct option added to the web.
- The correct answers are computer programmer and web site developer.

Q10.
Give a score of 0, 1, or 2 based on how well the answer meets the criteria listed below.
- The student should identify one reasonable lesson that can be learned from Mark Zuckerberg.
- The answer may refer to how he developed his talent, how he created something he believed in, how he remained true to himself during the process, or how he gives back to others.

Q11.
Give a score of 0, 1, or 2 based on how well the answer meets the criteria listed below.
- It should give a reasonable explanation of how the photograph and caption shows Zuckerberg's personality.
- It may be positive and refer to him as laid-back or humble or negative and refer to him as lazy or unprofessional.

Q14.
Give a score of 0, 1, or 2 based on how well the answer meets the criteria listed below.
- It should explain that the main problem that Troy has to overcome is that he is too short.
- It may refer to how Troy overcomes the problem by working harder, by having great ball skills, or by being faster.

Q17.
Give a score of 0, 1, or 2 based on how well the answer meets the criteria listed below.
- It should refer to Troy saying he would be the best player in the world and help the coach out one day.

Q19.
Give a score of 0, 1, or 2 based on how well the answer meets the criteria listed below.
- It should make a valid prediction about how the coach feels about his decision to give Troy a chance.
- The prediction could be that the coach is pleased, proud of his decision, or relieved that he made the decision.

Q20.
Give a score of 0, 1, or 2 based on how well the answer meets the criteria listed below.
- It should clearly explain why Troy's story is inspiring. The answer may refer to the message about not giving up on your dreams, about the value of hard work, or about how people can overcome barriers to achieve their dreams.

Q21.
Give a score of 0, 1, 2, or 3 based on how many correct examples are listed in the diagram. A sample answer is given below.
- He practices his ball skills longer than others. / He is fast and can get around others. / Players underestimate him.

Q22.
Give a score of 0, 1, or 2 based on how many correct supporting details are given.
- The student may refer to how he asks the coach for a chance, how he puts everything into the practice match, how he stays on the court to show his skills instead of taking a break, or how he works hard to develop his skills.

Q24.
Give a score of 0.5 for each word placed in the correct column.
- Synonyms: tiny, small, little, minute
- Antonyms: giant, massive, huge, great

Q26.
Give a score of 1 for each line that includes a reasonable explanation supporting the choice.
- The explanation for each line should describe how it shows the poet's opinion about how hardworking spiders are.
- Possible lines could include: I watch him as he toils, / Forever building come what may. / He builds his home to be the best. / Think how hard he has to toil, / Without a single word or moan.

Q28.
Give a score of 0, 1, or 2 based on how well the answer meets the criteria listed below.
- It should give a reasonable explanation of how stanza 3 has a message about overcoming disappointments.
- The answer should refer to how the spider does not get upset when his web is broken and simply starts again.

Q33.
Give a score of 0, 1, or 2 based on how well the answer meets the criteria listed below.
- It should give a reasonable explanation of what can be learned about hard work and determination.
- The answer may refer to keeping focused, to not complaining, to being determined to achieve a goal, or to working hard for your family or others.

Get to Know Our Product Range

Mathematics

Practice Test Books
Practice sets and practice tests will prepare students for the state tests.

Quiz Books
Focused individual quizzes cover every math skill one by one.

  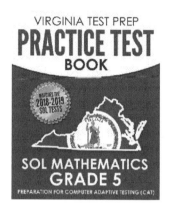

Reading

Practice Test Books
Practice sets and practice tests will prepare students for the state tests.

Reading Skills Workbooks
Short passages and question sets will develop and improve reading comprehension skills.

  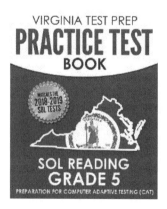

Writing

Writing Skills Workbooks
Students write narratives, essays, and opinion pieces, and write in response to passages.

Persuasive and Narrative Writing Workbooks
Guided workbooks teach all the skills required to write effective narratives and opinion pieces.

  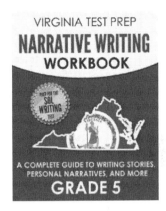

Language

Language Quiz Books
Focused quizzes cover spelling, grammar, writing conventions, and vocabulary.

Revising and Editing Workbooks
Students improve language and writing skills by identifying and correcting errors.

Language Skills Workbooks
Exercises on specific language skills including idioms, synonyms, and homophones.

http://www.testmasterpress.com

Made in the USA
Middletown, DE
30 September 2023

39835494R00071